Endorsements for
How the Gospel Brings Us All the Way Home

"While Christians may believe that the gospel merely begins our Christian lives, Derek Thomas shows us convincingly that the gospel is the beginning, middle, and end of our lives—indeed, that it is status-shaping, holiness-motivating, and glory-providing. Moving through the grand biblical themes of Romans 8 that shape our understanding of who and whose we are, believers will see that our union with Jesus determines everything about us. Would that my church members might marinate in these truths and so emerge gospel-soaked and gospel-encouraged."

—DR. SEAN MICHAEL LUCAS
Senior minister, First Presbyterian Church, Hattiesburg, Mississippi
Author, *What Is Grace?*

"In *How the Gospel Brings Us All the Way Home*, Derek Thomas skillfully expounds Romans 8, a passage that has become my favorite chapter of the Bible. Thomas dives deep into doctrinal truth and beckons us not only to believe these truths intellectually, but to experience the beauty of our personal salvation against the backdrop of the final restoration of all things."

—TREVIN WAX
Editor, GospelEPIC, LifeWay Christian Resources
Author, *Counterfeit Gospels* and *Holy Subversion*

"If asked, 'Which chapter of the Bible would you take with you to a desert island?' I suspect many believers would answer, 'Romans 8.' In a glorious section of God's Word, Paul sets before us the trials and the triumphs, the pains and the gains, the indicatives and the imperatives of living life as a child of God—saved by Christ, led by the Spirit, and cared for by a heavenly Father. Now, if a commentary on Romans 8 were permitted on the desert island, I would, without hesitation, recommend this wonderful exposition by Derek Thomas. Like the chapter it illumines so clearly, it is a literary treasure and a spiritual feast."

—DR. IAIN D. CAMPBELL
Pastor, Free Church of Scotland in Point, Isle of Lewis, Scotland
Author, *The Seven Wonders of the World:*
The Gospel in the Storyline of the Bible

"The best books are those that instruct the mind, engage the imagination, and ignite the heart with love for God. Dr. Derek Thomas' *How the Gospel Brings Us All the Way Home* does all three. With theological care, textual precision, and a pastor's heart, Dr. Thomas holds Paul's glorious meditation in Romans 8 to our eyes and helps us remember again just how great is the salvation Jesus won for His people. If you want a better understanding of the Bible, a deeper appreciation for the gospel, and a spur to worship Jesus Christ our Savior, this book is a great place to start."

—GREG GILBERT
Senior pastor, Third Avenue Baptist Church, Louisville, Kentucky
Author, *What Is the Gospel?*

HOW THE GOSPEL BRINGS US ALL THE WAY HOME

DEREK W. H. THOMAS

JR *Reformation Trust*   A DIVISION OF LIGONIER MINISTRIES, ORLANDO, FL

How the Gospel Brings Us All the Way Home

© 2011 by Derek W. H. Thomas

Published by Reformation Trust Publishing
a division of Ligonier Ministries
421 Ligonier Court, Sanford, FL 32771
Ligonier.org   ReformationTrust.com

Printed in Grand Rapids, Michigan
Color House Graphics
March 2012
Second edition, second printing

Cover design: Tobias' Outerwear for Books
Interior design and typeset: Katherine Lloyd, The DESK

Unless otherwise indicated, all Scripture quotations are taken from *The Holy Bible,
English Standard Version*, copyright © 2001 by Crossway Bibles, a division of Good
News Publishers. Used by permission. All rights reserved.

Scripture quotations marked NIV are from the *Holy Bible, New International
Version*®. NIV®. Copyright © 1973, 1978, 1984 by International Bible Society. Used
by permission of Zondervan. All rights reserved.

Library of Congress Cataloging-in-Publication Data

Thomas, Derek, 1953-
  How the gospel brings us all the way home / Derek W. H. Thomas.
      p. cm.
  Includes bibliographical references and index.
  ISBN 978-1-56769-256-3
  1. Bible. N.T. Romans 8--Sermons. 2. Presbyterian Church--Sermons. 3. Reformed
Church--Sermons. 4. Sermons, American. I. Title.
  BS2665.54.T46 2011
  227'.106--dc22

                                                      2011002685ß

To
Paul Stephenson
&
Don Breazeale

In loss,
they make Romans 8
incarnational

"No condemnation now I dread;
Jesus, and all in Him, is mine!"

From the hymn
"And Can It Be That I Should Gain"
by Charles Wesley (1738)

Contents

Foreword

There is an expression, "Horses for courses." It means that not everyone does everything equally well all of the time. For example, I have heard top-level professional golfers talk about the tournament courses they prefer because "they seem to suit my eye."

In the same way, if you are to purchase an entire book devoted to one chapter of the Bible, and that chapter is Romans 8, voted by acclamation to be among the greatest of all—profound in theology, soaring in eloquence, thrilling in impact—you don't want "just anybody" to be the author.

What, then, do you want? Probably someone with the ability to grasp the flow of Paul's logic; someone who is able to handle each text in its context; someone with a keen theological mind and a knowledge of the human heart; someone with long spiritual experience and the insight of years of studying Scripture and observing the Lord's ways; and someone who has music in his soul, who knows that the gospel sings, and who can reach both the low notes and the high ones.

If that is what you want in the author of a book on Romans 8, you have come to the right place—Derek Thomas is the author for you and *How the Gospel Brings Us All the Way Home* is the book for you. In these pages, Dr. Thomas brings all of the above characteristics to bear in a rich and wonderfully accessible exposition of this magnificent chapter of Scripture. In these pages, to transform some words of John Milton, "The hungry sheep look up and will be fed."

Derek Thomas is well known among Christians in the English-speaking world for three things. He is first and foremost an outstanding preacher; he is a learned and much-loved seminary professor; and he is the author of numerous books, many written for the "ordinary Christian," while others have been of special value to seminary students and scholars. The many aspects of his ministry, taken together, underline his sense that all of the gospel is for all of the people of God.

Among the best representatives of the Reformed theological tradition, of whom Derek Thomas is one, these three ministries — preacher, professor, author — are really one calling expressed in three ways — the fruit of an ongoing pursuit of, growth in, and sharing of the knowledge of God. When this knowledge is expressed in what our forefathers used to call a "feeling manner" — with pathos, spiritual affection, a passion for Christ, and a love for the people of God — the result is preaching, teaching, and writing that informs the mind, reaches the affections, bows the will in submission, and transforms the whole of life. Herein lies Dr. Thomas's special grace-gift, and the most obvious characteristic of this book.

It might be suspected that a foreword marked by such enthusiasm could be written only by a personal friend. I happily plead "guilty" to the charge of friendship with Derek Thomas, but that only adds to the pleasure any Christian will find in reading these pages. Over the thirty-five years we have known each other, I have often thought of the privilege it is to be able to count him as a friend, wise counselor, and fellow servant of Christ and His people. It is one of the very special blessings of belonging to the Christian brotherhood that one can admire the abilities of another without being consumed by jealousy because we all realize with Paul that we have nothing except what we have received from the Lord—so that we can rejoice in His gifts to others and not only to ourselves.

As you open these pages, you will find that Derek Thomas also becomes your good friend and trusted guide as he leads you through the glorious message of Romans 8, taking you from the joy and peace of "no condemnation" in the chapter's first verse to the assurance of "no separation" in the last verse. I count it an honor to commend these pages. But it is not in this page, but in the ones that follow, and in the way the gospel brings us all the way home, that you will find this book's best commendation, and the only one it really needs.

Now, as my parents sometimes would say to me as I left their presence when a teenager, "Just go, and enjoy yourself!"

—*Sinclair B. Ferguson*
First Presbyterian Church
Columbia, South Carolina
January 2011

Preface

The contents of these pages began as a series of sermons I preached at First Presbyterian Church in Jackson, Mississippi, during the summer of 2009. My friend (and boss), J. Ligon Duncan III, was granted a well-earned and (as was later evident) well-used sabbatical, and in his place I was asked to preach a series of Sunday morning sermons. I decided to preach a series covering the eighth chapter of Romans, a series I titled *The Best Chapter in the Bible*—a title remarkably similar, I later discovered, to one used by Dr. James Montgomery Boice of Tenth Presbyterian Church in Philadelphia.[1] Many of those who heard my sermons at the time commented on the profit they received, and some urged that I commit the series to book form.

Here it is—almost, for as every preacher knows, what "works" in a sermon does not always read as well, and the reverse is also true, perhaps more so. Consequently, even though the original sermons can be heard via the church's website,[2] there are aspects of this book that did not get preached.

No chapter of Scripture reaches the same sustained levels or covers the same ground as Romans 8. It is a description of the Christian life from death to life, from justification to glorification, from trial and suffering to the peace and tranquility of the new heaven and new earth. It contains exhortations to persevere as well as reassurances of God's preservation of His people. And no chapter has been cited more than this one in expounding the application of redemption in the life of an individual (the *ordo salutis*). In short, Romans 8 gives us a picture of salvation in its completeness. For this reason, I have titled this little book *How the Gospel Brings Us All the Way Home*.

Gratitude is the appropriate gospel response to grace received, and I am one to whom much grace has been shown in terms of my calling and vocation. I am especially grateful that, in addition to teaching systematic theology at Reformed Theological Seminary, I also serve as the minister of teaching at First Presbyterian Church in Jackson. The joy of serving alongside fellow ministers of the gospel in this historical church is incalculable, and the generosity of the church's senior minister is second to none. I am especially grateful for the warmth with which these sermons were received by the members and friends of First Presbyterian Church.

My life would be immeasurably poorer without the love and friendship of my wife, Rosemary. Although she owes me for her devotion to baseball, I owe her far more, and the hours spent in writing another book have meant baseball in one room and Romans 8 in another. I recall with great fondness the times when, struggling with Paul's phrase here and nuance there, I heard Rosemary shout at the TV when her beloved Atlanta Braves weren't playing according to her high standards. I do not share her love of baseball, but I love it that she loves it so. Her friendship over the past thirty-four years is an immense blessing.

I send this volume forth with the prayer that it might do the souls of those who read it much good. In particular, my longing is that these pages might rekindle a love for the gospel of Jesus Christ in our hearts. Truly, Jesus is the only hope we have and He is all we need.

—Derek W. H. Thomas
First Presbyterian Church/RTS
Jackson, Mississippi
Easter 2010

ROMANS 8:1–4

"There is therefore now no condemnation
for those who are in Christ Jesus.
For the law of the Spirit of life has set you free
in Christ Jesus from the law of sin and death.
For God has done what the law,
weakened by the flesh, could not do.
By sending his own Son in the likeness
of sinful flesh and for sin,
he condemned sin in the flesh,
in order that the righteous requirement
of the law might be fulfilled in us,
who walk not according to the flesh but
according to the Spirit."

GRACE AND GRATITUDE

(Romans 8:1–4)

"Guilty!" I can still hear that word as I close my eyes. It was 1975 in Oxford, England. I was passing by the city courthouse, where a murder trial was reaching its conclusion. The details were gruesome and the daily papers had carried detailed accounts of each day's court proceedings. I am not sure what made me attend the final day, but I did. I watched with fascination as the judge placed a black shawl on his head just before he pronounced the final verdict: "Guilty." A roar of approval erupted in the courthouse. The defendant was found guilty of murder and condemned to a life sentence with no possibility of parole.

Just as that man was found guilty in the judge's eyes, we are all guilty in God's sight: "None is righteous, no, not one . . . all

1

have sinned and fall short of the glory of God" (Rom. 3:10, 23).
Not a single human being is righteous by nature. No amount of
Christian or gospel influence makes people righteous. All people
are totally depraved—their motives, words, deeds, and thoughts
are affected by their identity as sinners. The natural inclination
of the heart, will, emotions, conscience, and physical body is in
an opposite direction to holiness. As J. C. Ryle said: "Sin . . . pervades and runs through every part of our moral constitution and
every faculty of our minds. The understanding, the affections,
the reasoning powers, the will, are all more or less infected."[3]

However, we are more than guilty; we are also condemned.
God justly pronounces a death sentence upon us.

Unfair? No, our "condemnation is just" (Rom. 3:8). We inherit
(through our identity with Adam) a sinful nature (cf. Rom. 5:16,
18). We sin because we *are* sinners. Apart from the gospel, our
guilt condemns us forever.

Freedom from Condemnation, Sin, and Death

However, the eighth chapter of Romans begins with the best news
imaginable: "There is therefore now no condemnation for those
who are in Christ Jesus" (Rom. 8:1). Charles Wesley celebrates
this truth in his hymn "And Can It Be That I Should Gain":

No condemnation now I dread;
Jesus, and all in him, is mine!

Alive in him, my living Head,
And clothed in righteousness divine,
Bold I approach th'eternal throne,
And claim the crown, through Christ, my own.[4]

"No condemnation now I dread"—that is what Paul is saying at the beginning of Romans 8. There is a way from condemnation to "no condemnation."

Similarly, Paul declares that Christians have been set free; they are emancipated: "For the law of the Spirit of life has set you free in Christ Jesus from the law of sin and death" (Rom. 8:2).

Christians have been set free from "the law." Paul is thinking of the law as a negative, imprisoning feature in our lives—and he is saying this after some fairly positive statements about the law in chapter 7:

- » "What then shall we say? That the law is sin? By no means! Yet if it had not been for the law, I would not have known sin" (Rom. 7:7).
- » "I agree with the law, that it is good" (Rom. 7:16).
- » "For I delight in the law of God, in my inner being" (Rom. 7:22).

In these verses, the apostle seems to be thinking about very positive ways in which the law functions in a believer's life. But in Romans 8:2, he is thinking of a different way in which the law functions—as a law of sin and death.

The need for perfect obedience

There are only two ways of salvation: by the law or by grace. If salvation is to happen by the law, perfect obedience is necessary. There can be no blemishes or shortcomings, for the law will never show mercy. It knows nothing of grace or forgiveness. It demands perfection, because whoever transgresses in one tiny detail transgresses the whole of God's law: "For whoever keeps the whole law but fails in one point has become accountable for all of it" (James 2:10). Getting to heaven through obedience to the law requires perfection. Merely doing your best will prove insufficient; good intentions are not enough. It is vitally important to grasp exactly how much the law demands if we think we are going to be in a right relationship with God through law-keeping. Simply put, "By works of the law no one will be justified" (Gal. 2:16).

For a brief season in his life, Jerome (ca. AD 347–420), the translator of the Bible into Latin (the Vulgate), decided to become a hermit, an ascetic. He went out into the desert, living among wild animals and scorpions. He became emaciated because of his extreme methods of fasting, trying to live by the standards of God's law as he understood it. He tells us in a biographical narrative that even as he was trying to conform himself to the standards of God's law, he found that his mind—even in the midst of a desert, while his body was wasting away—was filled with thoughts of the young girls who had surrounded him in Rome.[5] The law could not help him. In fact, the law exacerbated his sin. The law condemned Jerome. It was a law of sin and death.

4

Freedom through the Spirit

The law cannot bring life. Law-keeping is powerless to save. But the law *of the Spirit of life* can set us free. The Holy Spirit operates in such a way that He is able to set us free. In this opening section of Romans 8, Paul is saying, "Here is the gospel: the law of the Spirit of life says, 'There is a way for you to be free.'"

After twenty-seven years in prison, Nelson Mandela walked from his South African cell to freedom. He had spent ten thousand days in prison. "As I finally walked through those gates," he wrote, "I felt—even at the age of seventy-one,—that my life was beginning anew."[6] That is what Paul is saying in this verse. The Spirit of life sets believers free.

The law cannot put us in a right standing with God. It knows how to do only one thing: condemn us. It is relentless and unforgiving in this task. It is not because the law itself is sinful or desires our condemnation. The law says, "Do this and live," but we cannot. The problem lies in us, not in the law. The law is good but we are sinful. In other words, the law is "weakened by the flesh" (Rom. 8:3). It is not the law that is at fault. The problem lies in our inability to do what the law demands.

Roy Horn was part of the long-running two-man show "Siegfried & Roy" in Las Vegas. As part of the show, Horn performed with trained tigers. One day, Horn gave one of his tigers a command. The tiger refused to do it, so the ringmaster tapped him on the nose. Within seconds, the tiger grabbed Horn by the neck and dragged him around the ring. For several weeks afterward, Horn hovered between life and death.[7] This story reflects our relationship to the law: we think we are in control, but we are not. We are in bondage to the law.

The Way from Condemnation to Freedom

How, then, does Paul arrive at his conclusion that believers have moved from condemnation to "no condemnation," from sin and death to freedom? In other words, how can I be set free? How is it possible to find myself in a state of no condemnation? How can I tread the path of life rather than a path of death? These are among the most important questions we can ever ask ourselves.

The answer lies *outside* of our performance: "For God has done what the law, weakened by the flesh, could not do. By sending his own Son in the likeness of sinful flesh and for sin, he condemned sin in the flesh" (Rom. 8:3).

Notice two facets of this important truth. First, the initiative in our salvation comes from outside us: God (the Father) sent His Son. Our salvation is "not of blood, nor of the will of the flesh, nor of the will of man, but of God" (John 1:13). It is dependent on God's sovereign intervention and plan.

Second, our salvation depends entirely on what the Son did for us. Our salvation is dependent on Christ *alone*. It is not a cooperative venture, but one in which His accomplishments alone merit our salvation.

Christ in the likeness of human flesh

The way in which Paul phrases the coming of Jesus Christ into the world deserves some close attention. His language is precise.

Jesus Christ came "in the likeness of sinful flesh." Note what Paul does not (and cannot) say:

» He does *not* say that Christ came "in sinful flesh." Such a statement would call into question Jesus' sinlessness.

» He does *not* say that Christ came "in the likeness of flesh." Such a statement would question the reality of Jesus' incarnation, making Jesus to be an apparition or ghost-like figure (a view that some evidently did hold; see 1 John 4:2–3).

Jesus came as close to us as is possible, yet without sinning. He came enfleshed in sinless human nature to redeem us from our sin. He never sinned, but He was reckoned a sinner. By an act of substitution, He took *our* place. He came as the Lamb of God to offer Himself as a sacrifice for sin.

There was no other good enough
To pay the price of sin
He only could unlock the gates of heaven
And let us in.[8]

The title of Anselm of Canterbury's great work *Cur Deus Homo?* asked a fundamental question: why was it necessary for God to become man? Anselm answered the question by insisting that in order to represent God to us, Jesus had to be true God, and in order to represent us to God, He had to be true man. If we are to be saved from the consequences of our sin, the second person of the Trinity had to become incarnate and take our place. When Boso, a dim-witted character in Anselm's work, failed to understand why redemption required such an extravagant act, he was told: *Nondum considerasti, quanti ponderis sit peccatum* ("You have not yet considered what a heavy weight sin is").[9]

Believers found "in Christ"

However, Christ's work of redemption is not an impersonal act. Sinners must place their trust in Him and in what He accomplished for them.

When Paul writes, "There is *therefore* no condemnation" (v. 1, emphasis added) his "therefore" points to a conclusion based on something he has previously written. Take Romans 5:16, for example: "For the judgment following one trespass brought condemnation, but the free gift following many trespasses brought justification." Here, condemnation is contrasted with justification—a judicial declaration of righteousness. Two verses later, Paul writes, "as one trespass led to condemnation for all men, so one act of righteousness leads to justification and life" (Rom. 5:18). Again, condemnation is contrasted with justification.

When he comes to Romans 8, Paul appears to be picking up this theme again, putting it in the negative: in Christ, there is no condemnation. But he could have said it in the positive: in Christ, there is justification.

Our status in relation to Christ makes all the difference. Outside of union with Christ, we are guilty and condemned. But "in

Christ," we are declared not guilty (justified). Outside of Christ, there is only death (Rom. 5:12, 14, 17, 21); in union with Christ, there is "justification and life" (Rom. 5:18, 21).

This statement from Paul reminds us of something John Calvin wrote in the *Institutes of the Christian Religion*:

> We must understand that as long as Christ remains outside of us, and we are separated from him, all that he has suffered and done for the salvation of the human race remains useless and of no value for us. Therefore, to share with us what he has received from the Father, he had to become ours and to dwell within us.[10]

To know this condition of "no condemnation," Christ must "become ours and . . . dwell within us."

So we *can* move from "no condemnation" to "life." How? Paul's answer is characteristically precise and formulaic: we need to be "in Christ." All that Christ accomplished for us on the cross needs to be internalized. We must be brought into a living and personal relationship with Jesus.

The basis of the relationship

Given the universal, pervasive sinfulness of human beings, how can anyone ever be in a right relationship with God? More particularly, how can a human being ever be in a right relationship with a *holy* God? More particularly still, how is it possible for a just God to justify a sinner? That is one of the greatest questions we can ever ask.

9

To those with light views of sin, the justification of human beings may seem relatively simple to achieve. God is all-powerful, they conclude, and, after all, it is God's business to forgive.

Such trivializing of the issue signals the paucity of our understanding of who God is and what sin has done to our relationship with Him. God, Scripture declares, "will by no means clear the guilty" (Ex. 34:7; Nah. 1:3). The holiness of God requires that justice be done in clearing the guilty, something that cannot be accomplished merely by an act of God's will.[11]

Thus, the greatest issue of all time is the answer to the question that is before us: how is it possible for those who are guilty to be declared "not guilty"?

We come to Jesus Christ by faith, renouncing any confidence in our own ability to do anything worthy of God's salvation. Rather, we trust *only* in Jesus' sinless life, substitutionary death, and resurrection on our behalf. Every day, we must preach the gospel to ourselves and remind ourselves:

Nothing in my hands I bring
Simply to thy cross I cling.[12]

The problem of ongoing sin

Being "in Christ" does not stop a person from sinning. Paul alluded to the problem of ongoing sin in the life of a believer in the previous chapter: "I do not do the good I want, but the evil I do not want is what I keep on doing" (Rom. 7:19).[13]

Every Christian experiences the struggle of ongoing, remaining sin. Even in our very best efforts, we are conscious of the power of sin. The things we do are not done with the best of motives. The idol of self-adoration lurks behind everything we say and do, blemishing the deeds.

Worse than that, there are times when we fall headlong into sin. The power of temptation proves too great and our spiritual defenses too feeble, and we capitulate. Not a day, not an hour, not a minute or second passes without sin manifesting its ugly, unwelcome head. Even in the midst of worship, we find our minds wandering and our hearts engaged in something (or some-one) else. Our greatest sins occur in church.

Every Christian echoes Paul's lament and question: "Wretched man that I am! Who will deliver me from this body of death?" (Rom. 7:24). Listen to the frustration in Romans 7:

» "I do not understand my own actions" (7:15).
» "I do what I do not want" (7:16).
» "I have the desire to do what is right, but not the abil-ity to carry it out" (7:18).
» "I do not do the good I want" (7:19).
» "When I want to do right, evil lies close at hand" (7:21).
» "I see in my members another law waging war" (7:23).
» "Who will deliver me?" (7:24).

At every turn, our present reach exceeds our grasp. I will one thing, achieve another. "When will I ever be free from this corpse of sin?" Paul asks. Do you ask this question?

No new condemnation

The answer to the question, in part, is—*in heaven*. But Paul is seeking in Romans 8 to address another concern: Does the presence of sin in my life mean that I am not a Christian? Can I be in a right relationship with God (justified and adopted) and still sin as I do?

It is at this point that I so easily revert to a wrong way of thinking. I believe in Jesus Christ as Lord and Savior. I am saved from the penalty of sin. There is no condemnation. But then I sin again and I begin to think: "I must be condemned again. I need to try a little harder." So I go to church, read my Bible, sing more enthusiastically, and engage in spiritual thoughts about Jesus. Then I assume that I have slipped back into a state of "no condemnation" again. But tomorrow I sin again, and I slip back into a state of "condemnation." The cycle repeats itself over and over.

This performance mentality is all too common. Our status ("no condemnation"), our justification, our assurance of being "in Christ" is utterly dependent on our continuing (good) performance. I look to Christ for my justification, but I look to myself for my continued acceptance. It could not be more significant therefore that Paul—on the heels of the exasperation of Romans 7:14–25—utters the clearest word of assurance: "There is therefore now no condemnation for those who are in Christ Jesus" (Rom. 8:1). The issue is not, "Have I done enough good to outweigh my lack of performance?" On that account, I could never reach a state of assurance. Rather, the focus of our thinking must be, "Am I 'in Christ?'"

Even as mature Christians, we need to remind ourselves continually of the basis of our acceptance — it is entirely because of what Christ has done *for* us. Thus, faith in Christ is not a one-time event; we must live by faith each day.

The Response to Freedom from Condemnation

There can be only one proper response to grace: a life of grateful holiness. Christ's atoning death was "in order that the righteous requirement of the law might be fulfilled in us, who walk not according to the flesh but according to the Spirit" (Rom. 8:4).

There are two ways of understanding these words. One way is to view them as a statement of what our Lord achieved on the cross: He fulfilled what the law required by offering up a perfect obedience (the active obedience of Christ) and by meeting the law's retribution for our sin by His death (the passive obedience of Christ). He fulfilled the righteous requirements of the law for us in His life and death.

More likely, however, Paul is stating (what he will elaborate on later in this chapter) that Christians, whose sins are forgiven, now live in holy, obedient gratitude for the grace they have received. Grateful law-keeping is the saved sinner's response to received grace.[14] The rest of our lives are a way of saying, "Thank you."

Of course, salvation by grace rather than our performance can be seen as a license to sin (antinomianism). Paul's response in Romans is something like this: if we are not tempted to think

like that, we have not understood the gospel. The apostle anticipates our objection at the beginning of chapter 6: "Are we to
continue in sin that grace may abound?" (Rom. 6:1).

Grace *must* raise the temptation to think we can sin as we
please; if it does not, we have not understood the true extent of
grace. However, at no time can we yield to the temptation to
think this way (note Paul's answer to his question in 6:1 — "by
no means"), because Christians are called to a life of holiness —
holiness motivated by gratitude for all that God has done for
them in the gospel of Jesus Christ.

The key to subduing the downward drag of sin in our lives
is to know the impulse of gratitude that follows the experience
of forgiveness and reconciliation. Law-keeping out of love is the
true path of holiness.

For everyone "in Christ," there is no condemnation. What a
beautiful statement that is. Repeat it to yourself: "I have placed
my trust entirely in Jesus Christ and what He has accomplished
for me in His life, death, and resurrection. I am *in* Jesus Christ,
and there is no condemnation." What a sweet thing that is, what
a glorious thing.

A million questions arise, not the least of which is this: "How
can God possibly love me so much?" But the truth of the matter is
greater still: the blood of Jesus Christ has atoned for our past sins,
present sins, and even future sins. Whatever sin you may commit
tomorrow, there is no condemnation if you are in Jesus Christ.
They are blotted out.

Paul will have more to say about holiness, but it is important to see its foundation: received grace in the gospel of Jesus Christ, which declares sinners "Not guilty."

Grace—the grace that *is* Jesus—is breathtaking.

Do *you* agree?

ROMANS 8:5-8

"For those who live according to the flesh
set their minds on the things of the flesh,
but those who live according to the Spirit
set their minds on the things of the Spirit.
To set the mind on the flesh is death, but to
set the mind on the Spirit is life and peace.
For the mind that is set on the flesh is hostile to God,
for it does not submit to God's law; indeed, it cannot.
Those who are in the flesh cannot please God."

2

THE MIND'S DEFAULT SETTING

(Romans 8:5–8)

"Our thoughts are like the blossoms on a tree," John Owen muses. He goes on to say that many blossoms (thoughts) fall to the ground without producing fruit. However, some thoughts produce good or bad fruit. Owen then adds, "Ordinarily voluntary thoughts are the best measure and indication of the frame of our minds."[15]

Owen is asking: What do we think about when we are not thinking about anything in particular? What is the default setting of our minds if we just let them wander? The answers to these questions can tell us much about our spiritual condition.

Owen is reflecting on what Paul intends by the expression "to set the mind on the Spirit" in Romans 8:5 (or, as the New King

James Version puts it, "to be spiritually minded"). Those who have the Spirit live according to the Spirit and set their minds on the things of the Spirit; in other words, they set their minds on "things that are above." Those who do not have the Spirit live according to the flesh and set their minds on the things of the flesh; they set their minds on "things that are on earth" (Rom. 8:5; cf. Col. 3:1–2).

John Stott begins his book *Your Mind Matters* by saying that the major secret of holy living lies in the *mind*.[16] With this assertion, Stott reflects what Paul writes in the opening verses of Romans 8, but it is doubtful that many Christians would answer the question in this way.

Paul is concerned about the *content* of our thinking. His point is that what we think matters.

The apostle has two distinct types of people in mind: those who are *earthly* minded and those who are *spiritually* minded. Do you know which type you are? The promises of the gospel are given only to those who are spiritually minded.

Ask yourself these questions:

» What *naturally* comes to mind when I am not thinking about anything in particular?
» What is the default setting of my mind?
» Do I default to spiritual or worldly thoughts?

Two Mental Default Settings

How can we know whether or not our thinking is spiritual, whether our minds are set on the Spirit? In answering the question, Paul first draws attention to the mental preoccupation of those who live according to the flesh: "their minds are set on the things of the flesh." In other words, their thoughts are earthbound. Natural men think about earthly things. Their focus is on that which can be seen, heard, and felt.

While the term *flesh* can refer to the physical body (especially in the writings of the apostle John), Paul seems to have viewed the term in contrast with the Holy Spirit. In other words, the one who is "in the flesh" is not indwelt by the Holy Spirit. He is unregenerate and therefore still in union with Adam. Despite his best efforts and loftiest thoughts, he can never escape his nature; his thoughts remain earthbound. Those who are "in the flesh" are blind and insensitive to the beauties of the kingdom of God. Paul writes, "The natural person does not accept the things of the Spirit of God, for they are folly to him, and he is not able to understand them because they are spiritually discerned" (1 Cor. 2:14).

This blindness can be true even of those who spend their time in spiritual things. Jesus taught that apart from a *new* birth (regeneration), we cannot see the kingdom of God (John 3:3). Unless we have been born from above, we are simply unable to recognize spiritual realities. There is an amusing twist to the narrative: Jesus tells Nicodemus that a failure to understand spiritual things is a mark of those who are not born "from above." Nicodemus responds by saying, "I don't understand" ("How can these things be?" [John 3:9]). A Bible teacher Nicodemus may be, but without the Spirit, his understanding of Scripture remains earthbound.

Earthly mindedness equates to death

Things are worse than they seem. Those whose minds are earth-bound experience a kind of death (Rom. 8:6). We were made for greater things than gratifying the desires of the body or the Christ-less mind. Only Jesus provides complete satisfaction, fullness, integration, and fulfillment—what Jesus called "abundant life" (John 10:10), as opposed to spiritual death.

Spiritual blindness does not mean that non-Christians cannot achieve profound insight about the nature of reality or, on occasion, glimpse the transcendent. A Beethoven piano sonata, a painting by Rembrandt, a poem by Wordsworth—these are among the most sublime artifacts of human creation and have the capacity to reach beyond the authors' grasp. But none of these works can sit alongside the simplicity of the words in the prologue of John's Gospel: "In the beginning was the Word, and the Word was with God, and the Word was God" (John 1:1). Here we are on another level, a dimension to which the natural man has no access.

The unbelieving mind may soar into the heights and touch something of the transcendent in poetry, music, art, and scientific endeavor, but these are faint glimpses of something that lies beyond this world, unseen and untouched. God's "eternal power and divine nature . . . [are] clearly perceived" (Rom. 1:20), but the natural man (the man without the Spirit) spends his days denying what he knows.

One who does not have the Spirit does not necessarily and self-consciously say, "How can I destroy my life today?" He may choose a path that looks good and proper, but it leads to destruction: "There is a way that seems right to a man, but its end is the way to death" (Prov. 14:12). A relentless anti-God energy is at work in the minds of unbelievers, distracting, deceiving, and dragging down every thought into a grave.

The mind set on the Spirit

In contrast, the mind of the believer is set on the Spirit and spiritual things. Paul expresses this in different ways in Romans 8:

- » "The Spirit of God dwells in you" (v. 9).
- » "Christ is in you" (v. 10).
- » "The Spirit of him who raised Jesus from the dead [i.e., the Father] dwells in you . . . his Spirit . . . dwells in you" (v. 11).

To have Christ is to have the Spirit, because Christ indwells us by the Spirit. To mind the things of the Spirit is to mind the things of Christ, too. Knowing Christ this way is "life and peace" (Rom. 8:6). It is the peace of covenant benediction come to full maturity:

"The LORD bless you and keep you;
the LORD make his face to shine upon you and be
    gracious to you;
the LORD lift up his countenance upon you *and give you
    peace.*" (Num. 6:24–26, emphasis added)

The Heart of the Problem

Paul does not simply state the fact of our moral failure; he also addresses its cause: "The mind that is set on the flesh is hostile to God, for it does not submit to God's law; indeed, it cannot. Those who are in the flesh cannot please God" (Rom. 8:7–8).

Our natural inability to please God is because of a necessity of nature: the natural man, the man without the Spirit, the unregenerate man, *cannot* please God. Why is this so? The answer is simple. The earthbound, flesh-focused mind cannot please God because it is all about *itself*. It is self-centered. The unbelieving mind sets itself on the throne and says, "I am God." The unbelieving mind is therefore hostile to the one true God.

"Man's nature," John Calvin wrote, "is a perpetual factory of idols."[17] Our ability to create an idol and worship it knows no limit. Like Adam and Eve, we have come to doubt whether depending on and responding to our Maker is our true calling. We have believed the lie that suggests the farther we get from God the nobler we will be. Our natural self—the Adamic self—chooses and sets goals with a view to pleasing itself. It is our *nature* to behave in this way.

The natural man's constitution makes it impossible for him to do other than please himself. He cannot obey God's law from his heart. Enmity toward God, moral inability to please God, defection from God so as to mind the things of the flesh—these are instinctive to him. He cannot evade them. He is "*dead* in [his] trespasses and sins" (Eph. 2:1, emphasis added). He is not just sick or even terminally ill; he is *dead*.

Man's inability to do good

Is it true that the natural man cannot do *any* good at all? Is this not something of an overstatement? The Westminster Confession of Faith, for example, reflects this point of view when it asserts:

> From this original corruption, whereby we are utterly indisposed, disabled, and made opposite to all good, and wholly inclined to all evil, do proceed all actual transgressions.[18]

Are there not occasions when unbelievers show acts of kindness and self-sacrifice? Imagine, for a moment, writing a letter to one of the national newspapers in which you say, "Non-Christians have never done anything good." It would not be difficult to imagine the opprobrium that would result from such a statement. What, then, do Paul and the Westminster Confession mean when they collectively assert such a position?

The answer requires some finesse. Calvin, for example, taught that fallen human beings still have the capacity for what he called "civic virtue"—keeping laws and conventions of society, and interacting with others in a way that is not vicious or evil.[19] In these relationships, human beings are capable of acts that are good, compassionate, laudable, and virtuous. Indeed, non-Christians often prove kinder than Christians in acts of mercy and compassion.

Goodness as God sees it

How is this admission, that there exist acts of human kindness that we may label "good," compatible with Paul's assertion: "None is

righteous, no, not one. . . . No one does good, not even one"
(Rom. 3:10–12; see Ps. 14:1–3)? R. C. Sproul writes:

> The answer is that what fallen man can do on the horizon-
> tal plane in his behavior toward other people he cannot do
> on the vertical plane in his behavior toward God. When
> Scripture records, "There is none who does good, no, not
> one," *good* is more narrowly defined than it usually is.[20]

The "goodness" in view in Romans 3:12 (citing Ps. 14:3) is
goodness as God sees it. The Bible is asserting that even acts of
civic kindness done by an unbeliever fail to meet the requirement
of God's law — namely, that all our actions must be done with a
view to glorifying God. In that sense, even the unbeliever's good
acts are evil. These actions "cannot please God" (Rom. 8:8). In
the language of *The Book of Common Prayer* (1662), "there is no
health in us."

The unbeliever's moral inability to do good — good that may
be credited to his account by way of righteousness — means that
there is only one possible way of salvation: it must come from
outside himself. God alone can provide new life where there is
inability and blindness. We need a spiritual rebirth, one that God
alone can provide.

A Challenge to Our Self-Sufficiency

The emphasis on divine sovereignty and human inability chal-
lenges our native belief in self-sufficiency. The problem is that

our default setting is to rely on self-justification. However, there is no hope if all we have is a gospel of self-help, a "pick-yourself-up-by-your-bootstraps" mentality. All such schemes inevitably will end in failure.

Once we become aware of our sinful condition, divine sovereignty is all we have left—and what a gracious and wonderful thing it is to know that what we cannot do, God is both willing and able to do.

As believers, we dare not revert to an Adamic way of thinking—which can be summed up as "living according to the flesh." Having begun in the Spirit, we cannot now revert to the flesh for our sanctification and growth in grace (cf. Gal. 3:3). We cannot live other than "in the Spirit"—with our minds set on the things of the Spirit. We are called to squeeze out worldliness by a new love for Christ. It is a call to crucify "the flesh with all its passions and desires" (Gal. 5:24).

To "set the mind on the Spirit" (Rom. 8:6) is to walk "in step with the Spirit" (Gal. 5:25).

Here is a test:

»   When the Spirit's way—Christ's way—says, "Take the path of self-denial," do we respond by saying: "Self-denial is for wimps. I know my rights"? That's the earthly minded response.

»   When the Spirit's way—Christ's way—says, "Endure the trial; it will be good for you," do we respond by saying, "That's not fair; I deserve better than this"? That's the earthly minded response.

» When the Spirit's way—Christ's way—says, "I want you to glorify Me in everything you do," do we respond by saying, "This time it's going to be about me and only me"? That's the earthly minded response.

We are called to spiritual-mindedness. Sinclair Ferguson helps us here:

We are not naturally capable of loving God for Himself; indeed, we hate Him. But in discovering this about ourselves, and in learning of the Lord's supernatural love for us, love for the Father was born. Forgiven much, we loved much (Luke 7:47). We rejoiced in the hope of glory, in suffering, even in God Himself (Rom. 5:2, 3, 11). This new affection seemed first to overtake our worldliness, then to master it. Spiritual realities—Christ, grace, Scripture, prayer, fellowship, service, living for the glory of God— filled our vision and seemed so large, so desirable, that other things by comparison seemed to shrink in size and become bland to the taste.[21]

Quoting Thomas Chalmers, Ferguson adds: "The way in which we maintain 'the expulsive power of a new affection' is the same as the way we first discovered it. Only when grace is still 'amazing'—when we return to Christ and the cross where God's love for us was demonstrated to us (Rom. 5:8)—does it retain its power in us."[22]

Do not default to the mind's natural setting. Go back to where you began this journey of spiritual life—with an outstretched hand receiving grace, an eye fixed on Jesus, and a heart filled with wonder, praise, and adoration.

Do you hear the call to repentance?

ROMANS 8:9–11

"You, however, are not in the flesh but in the Spirit,
if in fact the Spirit of God dwells in you.
Anyone who does not have the Spirit of
Christ does not belong to him.
But if Christ is in you,
although the body is dead because of sin,
the Spirit is life because of righteousness.
If the Spirit of him who raised Jesus
from the dead dwells in you,
he who raised Christ Jesus from the dead
will also give life to your mortal bodies
through his Spirit who dwells in you."

3

SPIRITUALLY MINDED

(Romans 8:9–11)

A ssurance of pardon in this life implies security of life in heaven. That means Christians should die well. With this in mind, J. I. Packer relates the following incident:

> Three centuries ago a story went round about a student visit to Thomas Goodwin, the Puritan president of Magdalen College, Oxford. In the dark study Goodwin opened the conversation by asking if his visitor were ready to die. The lad fled. The story was told for laughs then, as it would be now; but it ought to be said that if it really happened, Goodwin was asking a proper pastoral question that should not be made fun of, whatever we might think

of his technique. For however old or young you are, one secret of inner peace and living to the full is to be realistically prepared for death—packed up, we might say, and ready to go. It is not absurd for us to remind each other of that fact.[23]

Christians have no need to be afraid of death, since "the Spirit of him who raised Jesus from the dead . . . will also give life to [our] mortal bodies" (Rom. 8:11).

The eighth chapter of Romans begins with the assertion that in Christ there is "no condemnation." The record of our sins has been wiped clean. Christians are reckoned as righteous as Christ is. Through faith in Christ alone, we are justified—reckoned to be in right standing with God. Our justification is an accomplished and present reality. Still to come, however, is its consummation, when believers will enter its eschatological dimension, when a "crown of righteousness [Greek, *dikaiosynē*, "justification"]" will be given to them (2 Tim. 4:8). As the Westminster Shorter Catechism says, "At the resurrection, believers being raised up in glory, shall be openly acknowledged and acquitted in the day of judgment."[24]

Believers—those who are spiritually minded (Rom. 8:6–7)—know life in its fullness, life now and life after death. Indeed, what we know now is but a foretaste of what is to come. We are those upon whom the end of the ages has already dawned (1 Cor. 10:11). As adopted sons of God, we wait eagerly for the next stage in our redemption, what Paul later in this chapter describes as our "adoption as sons, the redemption of our bodies" (Rom. 8:23).

No condemnation now (Rom. 8:1) and the promise of (bodily) resurrection to come (Rom. 8:11). It is a package deal, for nothing can separate the believer from his union with Christ (Rom. 8:39). In the application of redemption (*ordo salutis*), an inexorable link ties predestination in eternity to our calling into union with Christ, our justification, and our final glorification (Rom. 8:30). It stands to reason, of course, because if any possibility exists that a believer in union with Christ is not raised with Him at the end, *predestination* would have to be given an entirely different meaning.

Thus, every believer lives in a tension between what he is and what he will be, between the *now* and the *not yet*. And God the Holy Spirit is intimately involved in each stage:

Now—the Holy Spirit dwells in the body, giving life (Rom. 8:10).

Not yet—the Holy Spirit will raise the body to (resurrection) life (Rom. 8:11).

The logic is expressed elsewhere in a similar fashion: the presence of the Holy Spirit *in us* now is the "guarantee of our inheritance until we acquire possession of it" (Eph. 1:14).

The Spirit of Christ in the Believer

In Romans 8:9–11, Paul employs a variety of synonyms to express the indwelling of the Spirit:

» "in the Spirit" (v. 9)
» "the Spirit of God dwells in you" (v. 9)
» "the Spirit of Christ" or "Christ . . . in you" (vv. 9–10)
» "the Spirit of him who raised Jesus from the dead dwells in you" (v. 11)
» "his Spirit who dwells in you" (v. 11)

The interplay of the Spirit's indwelling and Christ's indwelling is both fascinating and revealing. While Jesus and the Holy Spirit are personally distinct, They are entwined with one another. The Spirit comes and makes His home in the hearts of those who believe in Jesus. The Spirit is "another Helper" like Jesus (John 14:16). He is "another" (Greek, *allos*) of a *similar* kind.[25]

The Spirit: Jesus' representative

It is important for us not to divorce the ministry of the Spirit and the ministry of Jesus. After all, the Holy Spirit is Jesus' personal representative agent in our hearts. The Spirit's ministry is to floodlight the ministry of Jesus and to seal His redemptive accomplishments to us.

How is the work of Christ as our substitute and sin-bearer applied to us? Answer: by the Spirit's work in calling, regeneration, justification, adoption, and sealing. The Spirit does nothing *apart* from the Father and the Son. In the words of the Patristic Fathers, the external operations of the Spirit cannot be separated from the other two persons of the Trinity (*opera Trinitatis ad extra sunt indivisa*).

In Romans 8:11, all three members of the Trinity are in view:

"If the *Spirit* of *him* [the Father] who raised *Jesus* from the dead dwells in you. . . ." This is why Paul can speak of "Christ . . . in you" (v. 10) and "the Spirit . . . in you" (v. 11). Later in this chapter, Paul will reflect on how the Spirit enables us to cry, "Abba! Father!" (v. 15).

A better "Helper"

In the upper room, Jesus gave considerable attention to the redemptive connection between Himself and the Holy Spirit. "It is to your advantage that I go away," Jesus told His disciples, "for if I do not go away, the Helper will not come to you. But if I go, I will send him to you" (John 16:7). The disciples were understandably fearful of losing the Savior's presence and fellowship. The truth was that they would come to know Jesus better *after* He had disappeared from this world.

Does the presence of the Spirit seem a poor substitute for the presence of Jesus *in the flesh*? Perhaps this thought occurred to the disciples in the upper room. But a moment's reflection dispels any such concern. The Holy Spirit was present at the conception of Jesus (Luke 1:35) and enabled Him to grow in wisdom, strength, and favor with God and with men (Luke 2:40, 52). The Spirit came upon Jesus at His baptism and thereafter acted as principal strategist in Jesus' encounter with the powers of darkness (Luke 3:22; 4:1). By the Holy Spirit Jesus offered His life on the cross as an atonement for sin (Heb. 9:14). And, as Paul reminds us in this passage, by the Spirit Jesus rose from the dead (Rom. 8:11).

To have the Spirit in our hearts is to have Him who has been intimately involved in every facet of Jesus' work—incarnation, obedience, sacrifice, and resurrection. And the Spirit has been in fellowship with the Son for eternity. The Spirit knows the Father and the Son in comprehensive, exhaustive detail. He searches "the depths of God" (1 Cor. 2:10). Nothing is hidden from the Spirit. He "proceeds" from the Father (John 15:26) and is breathed out by the Son (John 20:22). "By this we know that he abides in us, by the Spirit whom he has given us" (1 John 3:24). It is the Spirit who brings us into "fellowship . . . with the Father and with his Son Jesus Christ" (1 John 1:3).

The Believer "in the Spirit"

Paul can also turn the expression around and say that the believer is "in the Spirit." What does he mean?

The expression "in the Spirit" does not mean that we are "in the mood for" something. I may be in the mood for chocolate, Bach, or the Grateful Dead. But Paul means something much more significant than an occasional fancy. Thus, he does not intend the expression to suggest that believers are in the mood for religion (as we might convince ourselves that we are in the mood for prayer or reading the Bible).

Rather, what is in view is the dynamic relationship of the Spirit's indwelling. Just as it can be said that we are "in Christ" and "Christ dwells in us" (cf. Col. 1:2, 27), so it can be said that we are "in the Spirit" and "the Spirit dwells in us." These equally acceptable phrasings spell the mutual fellowship of the union of the believer and the Holy Spirit. We are in union with the Spirit and the Spirit is in union with us—and together we are in union with Jesus Christ and He with us.

This relationship is deeply mysterious; we cannot fathom its depths. The parallel is the mutual indwelling of the Father and Son: "the Father is in me and I am in the Father" (John 10:38). Each individual identity is preserved even as the closest possible fellowship is suggested.

A glorious privilege

Can we imagine a more glorious privilege than this? No.

One recent summer, in a large urn that sits outside the front door of my house, a blue swift made a nest in which she laid six eggs. This beautiful, shy creature had made her home in (almost) my house. I felt privileged that I had been honored by her presence, even if my cat viewed it entirely differently.

If I felt privileged when a bird nested by my door, how much more privileged should I feel knowing that the Holy Spirit has taken up residence in me? Our hearts should well up with gratitude and song at the mere thought of it. It is staggering.

Some of us take photographs when distinguished guests visit our homes. I love to glance through a "Visitor's Book" to see who has stayed in a home. On occasion I see the name of a well-known evangelical figure or a dear friend. But none of this compares to having the Spirit dwell permanently in our hearts.

Implications of the relationship

There are several important implications of our being "in the Spirit":

First, once we appreciate that the Spirit indwells us, we can never think of ourselves in the same way again. As soon as the Spirit comes, as soon as Jesus dwells in us, we are no longer the same as we were. "It is no longer I who live," says Paul, "but Christ lives in me" (Gal. 2:20). I am no longer the man in Adam but the new man in Christ. I am a "new creation" (2 Cor. 5:17). The implications of this are vast, and Paul elaborates on one of them in these verses by saying, "the Spirit is life" (Rom. 8:10).

By nature we are dead in trespasses and sins (Eph. 2:1), but "in the Spirit" we have been "made alive" (Eph. 2:5). Sin brought death into the world—"the body is dead because of sin" (Rom. 8:10)—but the promise of the Spirit is life—eternal life, resurrected life, bodily life in a new heaven and new earth. The Spirit is the guarantee of many things to come.

Second, every believer is a "temple of the Holy Spirit" (1 Cor. 6:19). This has implications for holiness—the call to mortify remaining sin "by the Spirit" will follow (Rom. 8:13). We are no longer to consider ourselves debtors to the flesh (Rom. 8:12). Sin and the Spirit ought not to live together, even if in this life they do—so much so that Paul could draw the shocking conclusion that so-called Christians engaging in sexual license in Corinth were in effect uniting Christ in prostitution (1 Cor. 6:15–17). "Glorify God in your body" because "your body is a temple of the Spirit" (1 Cor. 6:19–20).

Third, every other believer is also a temple of Christ by the Spirit and must be viewed as such. In this union with Christ by the Spirit there can be no prejudice according to race, color, education, or economic circumstance. These differences cannot affect my relationships with fellow believers in the gospel. "In Christ Jesus you are all sons of God, through faith. . . . There is neither Jew nor Greek, there is neither slave nor free, there is neither male nor female, for you are all one in Christ Jesus" (Gal. 3:26–28).

Life as Preparation for the Next Life

Our bodies are dying. This fact is true of every person in the world. Even the fittest body is dying. Sin brought this about. Knowing this prompted the Puritan Thomas Goodwin to ask his young student, "Are you ready to die?"

We (in the affluent West) live, for the most part, in a death-defying, live-for-the-moment-down-here culture. Our culture has sanitized death. Few people outside the medical and funeral professions come into regular contact with death. When death visits, many are unprepared for it, and consequently grief counseling has become a major industry of our time.

Christians, on the other hand, learn to view this life as a preparation for the life that is to come. In union with Christ by the Spirit, Christians learn to long for this life to pass so that the life to come—already promised in the gospel—becomes a reality. They learn to live, as the Puritans encouraged their flocks long ago, *sub specie aeternitatis* ("from the standpoint of eternity")—that is, in two-worldly terms, with life in this world viewed as a pilgrimage to the next. Christians must learn to view the death-encompassed life of the *now* as but a stage we pass through before life in its fullness dawns after death.

When life in its fullness dawns in the world to come, what will it be like? A resurrected physical body? Yes. A soul? Yes. A restoration of Eden—the blessings of the garden in which Adam and Eve lived, worked, and played? Yes. But much more, too. In view is a new order of existence—"we shall all be changed" (1 Cor. 15:51)—of which all that can be said at this stage is that "no eye has seen, nor ear heard, nor the heart of man imagined, what God has prepared for those who love him" (1 Cor. 2:9). Do not minimize what God has in store for Christians in the world to come.

The things that matter most

When James Dobson visited Graceland in Memphis, Tennessee, in 1997 and saw for himself the museum of "stuff" that once belonged to Elvis Presley, he gave the following reflection: "So what? So what if there are hundreds of tarnished gold and platinum records hanging side by side in the mansion? So what if RCA gave Elvis a trophy nine feet high and designated him the greatest entertainer of all time? . . . So what? It's all 'wood, hay and stubble' now."[26]

We may amass many things (toys) in the course of this life, but in the end, they will perish. But the gospel holds out before us the promise of eternal life.

In 1631, the Covenanter Robert Bruce (1554–1631) was sentenced to death for preaching the gospel. On the morning of his execution, his daughter cooked him an egg for breakfast. It was his request. (Who cares about his cholesterol level when he is about to die?) It was so nice, he said, that he almost asked his daughter to cook him another one. Then he paused and said to her, "I breakfasted with you this morning; I'll have supper with Jesus tonight."[27]

Robert Bruce was in the Spirit. The Spirit of Jesus dwelt in him. He knew how to live and he knew how to die.

A final warning

We have been asking the question: *if* the Holy Spirit indwells us, what then? But we also need to address another question: *if* the Holy Spirit *does not* indwell us, what then? It is a question Paul considers and answers. If you do not have the Spirit, he says, you are not His: "Anyone who does not have the Spirit of Christ does not belong to him" (Rom. 8:9).

Do *you* belong to Jesus?

ROMANS 8:12–13

"So then, brothers, we are debtors,
not to the flesh, to live according to the flesh.
For if you live according to the flesh you
will die, but if by the Spirit
you put to death the deeds of
the body, you will live."

- 4 -

KILLING FIELDS

(Romans 8:12–13)

M ost Christians, if they are honest, admit to failure when it comes to dealing with personal besetting sins. How is it with you? Do you tolerate them while inwardly wishing they would leave? Do you secretly pamper and feed your sins? (I say "secretly" knowing that we fool ourselves into thinking that there is such a thing as "secrecy," but in reality there is not: God sees and knows everything.) Or do you, perhaps, feel wholly inadequate to deal with your particular sins?

Consider these words:

The choicest believers, who are assuredly freed from the condemning power of sin, ought to make it their business all their days to mortify the indwelling power of sin.[28]

That was John Owen making the obligation to deal with sin clear and plain in what he termed a "discourse" on mortification. Written in the second half of the seventeenth century, his observations continue to help those who read his work. The book's genesis was a series of sermons that Owen preached to teenage boys at Oxford University. The text for this series of sermons was Romans 8:13, which, in the King James Version, reads, "If ye through the Spirit do mortify the deeds of the body, ye shall live." In view is the negative side of God's work of sanctification—*mortification*, which is the killing of remaining sin in us.

Mortification is a painful topic. As J. I. Packer reminds us, "When Rabbi Duncan told his students to read Owen's thoughts on mortification, he warned, 'Prepare for the knife.'"[29]

What prompted Owen to preach these sermons in the first place was a scenario all too common for every Christian:

Suppose a man to be a true believer, and yet finds in himself a powerful indwelling sin, leading him captive to the law of it, consuming his heart with trouble, perplexing his thoughts, weakening his soul as to duties of communion with God, disquieting him as to peace, and perhaps defiling his conscience and exposing him to hardening through the deceitfulness of sin,—what shall he do? What course shall he take and insist on for the mortification of this sin, lust, distemper or corruption?[30]

What are we to do with the sin that remains in us? The answer is simple: *kill it*. Killing sin, however, is never simple.

The Importance of Mortification

Mortification, or as the ESV correctly translates it, "[putting] to death the deeds of the body" (Rom. 8:13), means what it says: we are *not* to show sin mercy; sin is to be killed—outright.

There is to be no "peace" with sin. We dare not baptize our sins with benedictions. It is imperative that sin be destroyed. Its life is not to be spared. There must be a radical destruction of sin. Kill it; strangle it; starve it of oxygen until it cannot breathe again. There is no other way.

It is not just Paul who shows intolerance for sin. Do you remember Jesus' words in the Sermon on the Mount?

> "If your right eye causes you to sin, tear it out and throw it away. For it is better that you lose one of your members than that your whole body be thrown into hell. And if your right hand causes you to sin, cut it off and throw it away. For it is better that you lose one of your members than that your whole body go into hell." (Matt. 5:29–30)

"Tear it out." "Cut it off!" Without such radical action on our part, there can be no progress in Christian discipleship.

Paul makes a similar exhortation in his letter to the Colossians, where he gets specific about the sins he has in mind: "Put to death therefore what is earthly in you: sexual immorality, impurity, passion, evil desire, and covetousness, which is idolatry" (Col. 3:5). It is fascinating, isn't it, that in Paul's day, as in our own, the most prevalent sin has to do with sex.

43

We are in the midst of a war in which the enemy is sin—not just sin in general, but particular sins with names such as *lust, envy, pessimism, laziness, greed,* and *gossip*. We must show these enemies no quarter.

Can sins really be killed?

But is it realistic to talk this way about such things as lust or gossip? Are these not sins that we must learn to live with, hopefully tame a little, but not hope to conquer and destroy?

Past failure in dealing with some of our sinful habits has rendered some of us skeptical of making any real progress. It is not that we lack the desire to deal with sin; we simply lack confidence that there will be some semblance of success in the venture. We have tried to rid ourselves of this or that sin, but the success was short-lived. Past failures and the present *power* of particular habits and temptations lead us to pessimism—a defeatist outlook that cripples any hope of progress in holiness.

Has cynicism (a powerful force) rendered us content with a certain level of sanctification—one that lives at peace with occasional bouts of indulgence in sin—knowing that there is forgiveness in the atoning blood of Jesus Christ? Have the initial desires for holiness that followed our first love for Jesus grown cold?

Two responses need to be given to this way of thinking. First, by confession and repentance, there is indeed forgiveness for *every* sin. "If we confess our sins, he is faithful and just to forgive us our sins and to cleanse us from all unrighteousness" (1 John 1:9).

Second, assurance of forgiveness should never make us complacent and indifferent about sin. This complacency is what Paul anticipates in Romans 6 when he asks, "Are we to continue in sin that grace may abound?" (Rom. 6:1). The answer is decisive and precise: "By no means!" The spirit of antinomianism, whether derived from laziness in compliance with the law's demands or resignation because of our constant failure, is to be resisted.

A matter of life and death

The biblical admonitions to deal with sin are not made without hope of success. Indeed, Owen brought his discourse to a close with these words:

> Set faith at work on Christ for the *killing* of thy sin. His blood is the great sovereign remedy for sin-sick souls. Live in this, and thou wilt die a conqueror; yea, thou wilt, through the good providence of God, live to see thy lust dead at thy feet.[31]

Pause and read Owen's words again.

Once we give up the hope of victory, a deadly complacency sets in. Deadly? Yes, because for Paul mortification is a matter of life and death. There can be only one eventual victor. We either set about killing sin or sin kills us.

Perhaps we need to ask ourselves this question: have I killed a sin in recent memory? And if the answer is negative, we need to hear the Spirit's words:

» "If you live according to the flesh you will *die*."

» "If by the Spirit you put to death the deeds of the body, you will *live*."

It really is a matter of life or death.

The Role of Grace in Mortification

Paul's command to kill sin in Romans 8:13 reiterates an imperative in chapter 6: "Do not present your members to sin as instruments for unrighteousness, but present yourselves to God as those who have been brought from death to life, and your members to God as instruments for righteousness" (Rom. 6:13).

Imperatives—things we *must* do, with consequences if we do not—sometimes appear to some of us as graceless. "Do this and live" sounds like a return to a works-based, self-congratulatory religion. We are all wired for self-justification, so imperatives can feed into our need to do something in order to make ourselves a little more justified. "If only I can achieve a little more holiness," we sometimes say to ourselves, "God will be pleased with me again."

According to this view, we are saved by grace *alone*, but we are sanctified by our own effort. Our relationship with God, therefore, fluctuates from day to day in accordance with how well we perform. Maintaining our adopted relationship as sons of God (Rom. 8:14, 15, 19, 23) depends entirely on how well we do in killing sin. We say to ourselves, "He loves me, He loves me not; He loves me, He loves me not."

Keeping gospel principles before our eyes is essential if mortification is to be successful. Otherwise, we may find ourselves killing one sin and giving life to another—pride.

Unless our motivation in pursuing holiness is gospel-based and grace-centered, our efforts toward holiness become attempts to win God's favor. If we are not careful, we find ourselves adopting the spirit of the older brother in the parable of the prodigal son (Luke 15:11–32). Irritated by the grace shown to the prodigal son (for whom, upon his return, their father had thrown a party), the older brother protests: "Look, these many years I have served you, and I never disobeyed your command, yet you never gave me a young goat, that I might celebrate with my friends" (v. 29). The New International Version translation is very significant: "All these years I've been *slaving* for you . . ." (emphasis added).

Do you see what the older brother is saying? He views his obedience as "slavery." Thus, he views his father as his taskmaster.

Do you sometimes find yourself thinking of God as a hard taskmaster to be obeyed rather than a heavenly Father who loves you more than you can possibly imagine?

When counseling couples whose marriages are in trouble, I sometimes hear a spouse complaining: "I want him/her to do this for me because he/she *loves* me, not simply out of a sense of duty." Our motivation in obedience makes all the difference in a relationship.

Motivations to holiness

What is our motivation in pursuing holiness? Perhaps, to be more accurate, we should ask: what are our motivations (plural) in pursuing holiness? There is more than one motivation for holiness in the New Testament. In Romans 8, for example, the following two motivations are readily discernible:

» *I want to live and not die.* "To set the mind on the flesh is death, but to set the mind on the Spirit is life and peace" (Rom. 8:6). The principle here is, "We reap what we sow." If we yield to sinful desires, we will reap death. Too often, we fail to see the *long-term* consequences of our actions. We live for "now" without sufficient attention to the ultimate consequences of what we do. Sometimes all we can see is the fleeting enjoyment of the present; we hide from ourselves the truth that sin's payback ("wages," Rom. 6:23) is death.

» *My sin affects others in the church.* Several considerations underline this point: "brothers" (v. 12); the plural "you" (v. 13), showing that we belong to the family of God; and the affirmation that "all who are led by the Spirit of God are sons of God" (v. 14). Sinclair Ferguson writes, "Our fellowship with other Christians is one of the chief instruments God has given us to overcome sin."[32]

At a tender moment in my teenage years, when I had done something in school and the headmaster had chastised me for it, my older brother pulled me aside and said, "You have let the family down!" I had forgotten that I was a member of the Thomas family. His reminder was a powerful motivation designed to bring home to me the severity of my action and the disgrace caused to the family name.

Avoiding the legalism trap

How is it possible to be motivated by these principles and *not* view them in a purely legal fashion?

The word *legalism* is overused. Sometimes I tell my students at the seminary where I teach that they may use this word once a year and no more. All too often *legalism* is employed whenever we consider obedience inconvenient. *Legalism* then becomes a "scare tactic word" masking an underlying indifference or mistrust of radical holiness.

What does *legalism* really mean? It is the proper word whenever one of the following is true:

» I am being asked to obey *in order* to win God's favor. A works-based view of salvation is essentially legalistic.

» I am being asked to obey a command over and above that which God has given to me in the Bible. Essentially, I am being asked to obey *against* my conscience, which is subject to Scripture alone. "All members of this church must refrain from growing facial hair," for example, is an example of legalism.

» I am obeying God's commandments *from impure motives*. When the older brother in the parable of the prodigal son viewed his obedience as a form of slavery, his obedience was legalistic.

Is obeying from a consideration of gain—reaping life through actions of mortification—a form of legalism? Yes, if we think that Paul is teaching us that "life" is the reward given to those who put sin to death. But Paul is not saying that. Life is the *fruit*, not the *root*, of justification.

First, Paul is not saying that our efforts toward holiness are the basis on which we will be granted eternal life. That would violate everything Paul says about the basis of our salvation: "For by grace you have been saved through faith. And this is not your own doing; it is the gift of God, not a result of works, so that no one may boast" (Eph. 2:8–9).

Some will agree that we are saved initially by grace but then argue that our ongoing salvation depends on our works. Paul encountered this idea in the Galatian churches: "Did you receive the Spirit by works of the law or by hearing with faith? Are you so foolish? Having begun by the Spirit, are you now being perfected by the flesh? Did you suffer so many things in vain—if indeed it was in vain?" (Gal. 3:2–4). Our salvation, from beginning to end, depends entirely on the grace of God. In the songs heard in heaven, there is only One who receives the credit for the salvation of sinners: "Worthy are you . . . for you were slain, and by your blood you ransomed people for God" (Rev. 5:9). Who is He? He is Jesus, "the Lion of the tribe of Judah, the Root of David" (Rev. 5:5).

Second, Paul is saying that all progress in holiness is "by the Spirit" (v. 13). As he puts it elsewhere: "Work out your own salvation with fear and trembling, for it is God who works in you, both to will and to work for his good pleasure" (Phil. 2:12–13).

Holiness is never achieved by our unaided efforts alone. Neither should we view it as a process of equal cooperation, imagining that God works 50 percent and we work 50 percent, as though we are partners with God in sanctification. True, sanctification (our perseverance to the end) does not take place over our heads. But our holiness is achievable only because God works in us. The relationship between what we do and what God does is asymmetrical. Without God's work *in* us, we cannot do anything.

The Role of Our Identity in Mortification

What we need in order to engage in biblical holiness is a right understanding of who we are. As Ferguson puts it, in order to kill sin, we need to "go back from the *point of action* to a point from which we can *gain energy* for the strenuous effort of dealing with sin."[33] We need to go back to the point of our new identity in Christ. We need to ask ourselves, "Who am I?"

Every Christian has a new identity. Who does the word *you* refer to in the statement, "if . . . you put to death the deeds of the body" (v. 13)? It refers to Christians. And Paul has been spending a lot of time telling us what a Christian is.

Christians are no longer "in Adam" but "in Christ"; no longer in the flesh but in the Spirit (Rom. 5:12–21; 8:9). Perhaps nowhere is this put more succinctly than in 2 Corinthians 5:17. If anyone is in Christ, Paul says, "he is a new creation" (literally, "If anyone in Christ—new creation"). As Christians, we belong to a new order of existence. We are those upon whom the "end of the ages" has come (1 Cor. 10:11).

Several things emerge from this new existence of ours:

» We have "died with Christ" (Rom 6:8; Col. 3:3); we have been baptized into Christ's death (Rom. 6:3) and buried with him (Rom. 6:4; Col. 2:12); "our old self [better, "old man"] was crucified with him in order that the body of sin might be brought to nothing" (Rom. 6:6).

» We have been delivered from the *reign* of sin ("sin will have no dominion over you," Rom. 6:14). We have "died to sin" (Rom. 6:2).

» We have been baptized into Christ's resurrection: "Christ was raised from the dead by the glory of the Father, [that] we too might walk in newness of life" (Rom. 6:4). We have been "raised with Christ" (Col. 3:1); we have been "raised . . . up with him and seated . . . with him in the heavenly places" (Eph. 2:6).

» Our life is "hidden with Christ in God" (Col. 3:3).

» What is true of us *now* will be true of us *then*, or, more poignantly, what will be declared of us *then* is *already true of us now*: "Just as Christ was raised from the dead . . . we shall certainly be united with him in a resurrection like his" (Rom. 6:4–5; cf. Col. 3:4).

If we forget who we are, we will fail to be what we should be. And that is our biggest error—a failure to remember who we are *in Christ*. Here is John Stott's counsel:

The first great secret of holiness lies in the degree and the decisiveness of our repentance. If besetting sins persistently plague us, it is either because we have never truly repented, or because having repented, we have not maintained our repentance. It is as if, having nailed our old nature to the cross, we keep wistfully returning to the scene of its execution. We begin to fondle it, to caress it, to long for its release, even to try and take it down again from the cross. We need to learn to leave it there. When some jealous, or proud, or malicious, or impure thought invades our mind we must kick it out at once. It is fatal to begin to examine it and consider whether we are going to give in to it or not. We have declared war on it; we are not going to resume negotiations. . . . We have crucified the flesh; we are never going to [with]draw the nails.[34]

Sin is *inconsistent* with this new identity. Keep on telling yourself: "I am a Christian in union with Christ and I have no need to obey sin's demands any more. I am no longer sin's slave. I have been freed. I am a new creation."

Christian, you belong to Jesus Christ.

You bear His name.

You belong to a new order of existence.

Live in a way that honors these truths.

ROMANS 8:14–17

"For all who are led by the Spirit of God
are sons of God. For you did not receive the spirit
of slavery to fall back into fear,
but you have received the Spirit of adoption
as sons, by whom we cry, 'Abba! Father!'
The Spirit himself bears witness with our spirit
that we are children of God,
and if children, then heirs—heirs of God
and fellow heirs with Christ,
provided we suffer with him in order
that we may also be glorified with him."

5

SONS OF GOD

(Romans 8:14–17)

"The revelation to the believer that God is his Father is in a sense the climax of the Bible," writes J. I. Packer.[35] Being able to call our Creator and Redeemer "Father"—and to be called "sons" and considered as members of the family in which Jesus is our "elder brother"—is the difference between living under the old covenant and living in the new. Being able to say, "Abba! Father!" (Rom. 8:15; Gal. 4:6) is the heart of Christianity and our greatest privilege.

I once spoke to a father who had adopted a little child. In the initial months, things had gone well, but when this little girl came up to him and said, "Daddy, can you help me with my shoelaces?" he broke down with emotion. It was the first time she had ever used the word *Daddy*, and she used it in a way that seemed instinctive and natural. She viewed him as her father.

Christians can do just what that little girl did. We have "access . . . to the Father" (Eph. 2:18), for we are "children of God" or "sons of God" (Rom. 8:14, 16, 19, 21), having been adopted by God through the work of the Holy Spirit.

The application of redemption in us engages all three persons of the Trinity: we come "in Christ" (Rom. 8:1), by the Spirit (Rom. 8:14, 15, 16), to the Father (Rom. 8:15). As we saw in chapter 3, this illustrates a Patristic maxim: all persons of the Trinity share in all external acts of God (*opera Trinitatis ad extra sunt indivisa*).

But it is also possible to distinguish particular actions of the persons of the Trinity. The individual persons *appropriate* particular functions, and the Spirit appropriates adoption to such an extent that He is called "the Spirit of adoption" (Rom. 8:15). The Holy Spirit plays a major role in our adoption.

The phrase "the Spirit of adoption" occurs only once in the New Testament. Nevertheless, John Calvin was bold enough to suggest that "the Adopter" was the first title of the Spirit.[36]

In Romans 8:14–17, Paul emphasizes several aspects of the Spirit's work in our adoption as "sons of God."

Adopted to Holiness

The Holy Spirit is *holy*. He is the "Spirit of holiness" (Rom. 1:4). The goal of our regeneration by the Spirit is transformation into the likeness of Jesus Christ (Rom. 8:29). Thus, it is our holiness that is in view in Romans 8:14: "For all who are led by the Spirit of God are sons of God."

But where is there any mention of holiness in this text? The answer lies in the Spirit's "leading."

Tempted as we might be to consider the Spirit's leading as referring to guidance for vocation ("Is the Spirit leading me to change jobs?") or matrimony ("Is the Spirit leading me to marry him/her?"), this is not what Paul has in view. Paul is justifying the conclusion he drew in verse 13, that putting sin to death by the power of the Spirit leads to life. Lest we think the apostle has reverted to a works-righteousness view in which we earn our salvation by acts of mortification, in verse 14 he stresses the "indicative." We engage in mortification because ("For," Greek, *gar*) we are those who are (note the passive) "led by the Spirit of God."[37]

Under the Spirit's control

Christians are led by the Spirit; their entire lives are under the control of the Spirit. Paul is providing us with a definition: a Christian is one who is led by the Spirit. The great life-changing event (regeneration, being "in Christ" as opposed to being "in Adam") is marked by the Spirit's leading us to mortify sin and pursue Christlikeness.

Instead of a preoccupation with issues of guidance (*the* preoccupation of our era), we should be concerned to ask the Lord:

» "How can I live in a way that reflects the holiness of my Savior?"

> » "Will You show me how to deny myself?"
> » "Which sin, or part of a sin, am I to kill today?"

Easy believism—the view that we can confess with our mouths that Jesus is Lord without the engagement of our hearts (cf. Rom. 10:10)—is outlawed by what Paul writes here in Romans 8. All true Christians engage in a self-denying lifestyle, involving active participation (cooperation) with the Spirit in killing indwelling sin.

A two-sided course

Mortification is the negative side of a double-sided course of action. In addition to killing sin (death), there must be a corresponding rising to new life: "We were buried therefore with him by baptism into death, in order that, just as Christ was raised from the dead by the glory of the Father, we too might walk in newness of life" (Rom. 6:4). Older theologians called this twofold process mortification (*mortificatio*) and vivification (*vivificatio*). Sin needs to be resisted and destroyed; also, graces (the "fruit of the Spirit," as evidenced in Gal. 5:22–23) need to flourish, giving evidence of a resurrection.

Killing sin and pursuing holiness are acts of the Holy Spirit in cooperation with the believer. Christians "live by the Spirit" and "walk by the Spirit" (Gal. 5:25). The verb translated as "walk" could be rendered "keep in step with," suggesting a military style of synchronous marching.[38]

Are you marching in step with the Holy Spirit?

Adopted to Freedom

The Spirit's presence makes all the difference as to how we view these exhortations to holiness. His presence ensures that we are no longer slaves serving a hostile master: "You did not receive the spirit of slavery to fall back into fear" (Rom. 8:15). The New Living Translation paraphrases this verse in this way: "You should not be like cowering, fearful slaves."

Paul's aim is to emphasize that in receiving the Spirit, we have been designated sons. Not *slaves* but *sons.*

We considered earlier the possibility that our view of God may be more like that of the older brother in Jesus' parable of the prodigal son. He was angry with his father for showing such lavish attention and kindness when the errant brother returned. Had he—the older brother—not always been there, *slaving* for his father (Luke 15:29, NIV)?

Christians are no longer slaves. We must never think of our service for our heavenly Father as a form of slavery. Our obedience to Him must always come from thankful hearts. We gladly and willingly give our Father whatever He asks of us precisely *because* He loves us.

The "Spirit of slavery"?

Why does Paul raise the issue of slavery here at all?

Paul may be thinking of the way the Spirit first operates in hearts as we are drawn into union with Christ. Note how he contrasts the "spirit of slavery" and "Spirit of adoption":

"You did *not* receive the spirit of slavery to fall back into fear, but you *have* received the Spirit of adoption as sons." (Rom. 8:15, emphasis added)

An important and difficult issue emerges here: Why do the translators use lowercase to render "spirit of slavery" but uppercase for "Spirit of adoption"? Should it not also be "Spirit of slavery"?

How is the Holy Spirit a "Spirit of slavery"? Our first encounter with the Spirit's ministry is conviction of sin: Jesus told His disciples that when the Spirit came, He would "convict the world concerning sin and righteousness and judgment" (John 16:8). Is Paul thinking of his own experience subsequent to his encounter with the risen Savior on the Damascus Road before full assurance as to his new identity in Christ had matured? If so, does the apostle intend to suggest that this is an experience that all Christians share to some degree: the Spirit convicts us as to our sin and inability (making Him "the Spirit of slavery") and subsequently grants us assurance of our adoption through faith in Christ alone ("the Spirit of adoption")?

Confirmation of this interpretation of the Spirit as "the Spirit of slavery" can be found in the use of the word *again* (Greek, *palin*), left untranslated in the English Standard Version but included in the King James translation: "For ye have not received the spirit of bondage *again* to fear" (emphasis added). If Paul is suggesting that we do not currently experience the Spirit in this way, is he suggesting that at one time we did?

In the Presbyterian Church of Scotland, it was customary

among some elders of the church to ask a candidate seeking communicant membership the following question: "Have you been to Sinai?" They were not trying to ascertain whether the person had visited the Sinai Peninsula in the Middle East. Rather, they were asking whether the law (the moral law, or the Ten Commandments) had done a work of conviction in the person's heart. Did the candidate know anything of a release from bondage? Christians sing:

My chains fell off, my heart was free,
I rose, went forth, and followed thee.[39]

Many commentators do not view the bondage as caused by the Holy Spirit and insist that Paul is saying that Christians have not received the Spirit in this way at any time.[40]

Pointing to the Son and the Father

What is indisputable is that when the Spirit comes to make His home in us, He comes with grace in both hands. He comes to point to the Son and the extravagance of what has been accomplished for us. He introduces us to the Father in heaven and says: "Meet the Father. He is *your* Father, too."

How do you view your present relationship to God? Do you see it as one of slavery, a never-ending attempt to win some favor from an otherwise reluctant Father, or one in which you are a son, knowing that your Father in heaven has always loved you and always will.

Service in the kingdom of God is never to be viewed as a form of slavery. It is to be willing service engaged in from a heart that has fallen in love with the One who first loved us.

Adopted to Sonship

The Spirit bears the title "the Spirit of adoption" (Rom. 8:15). He fulfills the purpose of Jesus' coming into the world: "that we might receive adoption as sons" (Gal. 4:5).

Our adoption into God's family grants us *more* than that which justification provides. Hypothetically, it is conceivable that a person could be reckoned as being in a right relationship with God (free from condemnation) but not given the status of "heir of God" (cf. Rom. 8:17). It is conceivable that God *could* grant justification *without* the grace of adoption. After all, judges regularly declare a person "not guilty" without adding, "From now on, I regard you as my son and heir."

What are the blessings of adoption? The Westminster Confession lists several, including:

» new liberties and privileges
» access in prayer to the throne of grace with boldness
» understanding God to be a tender Father, whom we call "Abba"
» assurance of pity, protection, provision, and perseverance[41]

I once witnessed an endearing moment in the streets of Jerusalem as a devout Jewish father and his small son were making their way to the Wailing Wall. The Jewish Shabbat had begun and the man was walking with some haste—too much haste for the ability of his little son to keep up. With every other step the boy would cry, "Abba, abba!" Eventually, the boy's father stopped and bent over to lift his son and carry him.

That sort of scene is commonplace, of course. But the poignant sound of the cry "Abba, abba!" made me think of my relationship to my Father in heaven. I need only cry out to Him, and He listens to me and gladly helps me. I am His son. He is my heavenly Father. He will deny me nothing if I truly need it. I need only to ask Him for it.

A title with greater intimacy

But why not call God by His covenant name, "LORD," which, when capitalized in our English Bibles, represents the Hebrew "Yahweh" (Jehovah). This is God's proper name, the one He gave to the Israelites (Ex. 3:15). It is a form of the verb "to be." God explains the connection, telling us that His name means "I AM WHO (or WHAT) I AM" (or "I will be who I will be," Ex. 3:14ff). It signifies, among other possibilities, God's self-existence, eternality, and sovereignty.

Why did Jesus reply to the disciples' request for help in prayer by saying, "Pray . . . like this: 'Our Father in heaven . . .'" (Matt. 6:9)? He could have taught them to pray by saying, "Our LORD in heaven . . . ," but He did not.

Jesus died on the cross in order to grant us the privilege of calling God "Father." It is a title that spells a greater intimacy than God's covenant name.

A Father who hears our cries

The verb Paul uses to describe what Christians do is important: they *"cry,* 'Abba! Father!'" Sinclair Ferguson explains:

> This astonishing use of child-language ("Father") is so remarkable that it has sometimes obscured the force of Paul's teaching; for the verb he uses, "cry" (*krazein*), is powerfully onomatopoeic and indicates the presence of intense feeling. It is used in the Septuagint of loud cries and intense emotion (Job 35:12; Ps. 3:5, LXX), and similarly in the New Testament of the screaming of the Gerasene demoniac (Mk. 5:5), the shrieks of the spirit who possessed the epileptic boy (Mk. 9:26), the cries of Blind Bartimaeus (Mk. 10:47–48) and the cry of Jesus on the cross (Mt. 27:50). The atmosphere here is not tranquility but crisis.[42]

When our hearts are filled with terror and alarm, and we cry "Abba! Father!"—perhaps questioning the goodness of the providence our Father has unfolded—He hears us. He hears us when we are at our lowest points emotionally and spiritually. Can you think of anything more wonderful and glorious than knowing that your heavenly Father cares about you?

Adopted to Assurance

The Holy Spirit is the Spirit of holiness. He is the Spirit of freedom. He is the Spirit of adoption. He is also the Spirit of assurance:

"The Spirit himself bears witness with our spirit that we are children of God" (Rom. 8:16).

How does the Spirit bear witness with our spirit? Is the testimony that He gives direct or indirect, immediate or mediate? This is a matter that has divided Reformed theologians. The Puritans Richard Sibbes and Thomas Goodwin, for example, argued (to different degrees) that the Spirit's witness is felt directly upon the human spirit ("like a kiss," Sibbes suggested).[43] John Owen, at least in his mature writings, expressed the strong conviction that all witness by the Spirit comes mediated through the Scriptures.[44]

But perhaps the witness needs to be understood differently. It is in the *crie de coeur*, "Abba! Father!" that the Spirit is a witness. The testimony of the Spirit is then viewed epexegetically of the statement made in the previous verse.

Those who are not Christians rarely, if ever, call God "Father." They are far more likely to say, "O God." For Christians, it is different. In moments of doubt and weakness, the Christian's spirit cries out, "Father!" The very cry itself is testimony (the Spirit's testimony *with* us) of a work of grace in the heart. It is the reawakening of assurance. Amid troubled waters, a safe haven is discovered in the arms of a listening, waiting, loving, embracing Father.

"Abba! Father!"—this cry issues from the human spirit in Romans 8. In Galatians, the cry comes from the Spirit Himself: "Because you are sons, God has sent the Spirit of his Son into our hearts, crying, 'Abba! Father!'" (Gal. 4:6).

We cry. The Spirit cries. The Holy Spirit cries with our spirit (Rom. 8:16). This communion between us and the Spirit is the surest indication of our adoption as sons of God.

ROMANS 8:18–25

"For I consider that the sufferings of this
present time are not worth comparing with
the glory that is to be revealed to us.
For the creation waits with eager longing
for the revealing of the sons of God.
For the creation was subjected to futility,
not willingly, but because of him who subjected it,
in hope that the creation itself will be set free
from its bondage to decay
and obtain the freedom of the glory of the
children of God. For we know that the whole
creation has been groaning together
in the pains of childbirth until now.
And not only the creation, but we ourselves,
who have the firstfruits of the Spirit,
groan inwardly as we wait eagerly for adoption
as sons, the redemption of our bodies.
For in this hope we were saved.
Now hope that is seen is not hope.
For who hopes for what he sees?
But if we hope for what we do not see,
we wait for it with patience."

6

GLORIOUS HOPE

(Romans 8:18–25)

A s I write these lines, the headlines in the newspapers are familiar enough — typical, in fact, of any newspaper on any given day. Same old, same old:

- » Three people are missing and presumed dead following a landslide in a town just southwest of Berlin.
- » The controversial drug Thalidomide does not improve survival rates of patients with a certain form of lung cancer, according to a study.
- » More than a hundred people have been quarantined in China because of an outbreak of suspected swine flu.
- » The southern elephant seal is in danger of extinction, one of more than forty-four thousand threatened species on the planet.

Death, disease, disaster, and despicable behavior against animals—these are the norm in a world gripped by sin, cursed by Adam's fall in Eden.

Singer Johnny Cash, who was known for his signature black attire, sang these lines:

> I'd love to wear a rainbow every day,
> And tell the world that everything's OK;
> But I'll try to carry off a little darkness on my back,
> 'Til things are brighter.
> I'm the Man in Black.[45]

Creation, too, seems to be wearing black, according to the picture in Romans 8:18–25. The world is fractured; it is not what it was meant to be or what it one day shall be. The universe groans.

How did Paul get to the subject of a fractured cosmos? He has just written that Christians are sons of God and, together with Christ, heirs of glory (Rom. 8:16–17). This glory is a long way from the present world, with all of its afflictions and sorrows, so Paul seems to want us to lift our eyes above the shadows and help us glimpse the glory that is coming—yes, *coming*. What kind of glory? Answer: the glory that is the new heaven and new earth (cf. Isa. 65:17; 66:22; 2 Peter 3:13).

The Vanity and Misery of Life

For the present, that glory is a hope and not a reality. More accurately, the glory has dawned (in Christ, each of us is a "new creation," 2 Cor. 5:17) but has not reached maturity. The fullness will appear only on the other side of present suffering.

Meaninglessness pervades this present existence. As Qoheleth (the Preacher in Ecclesiastes) writes, life "under the sun" (in a world without God) is "vanity" (Eccl. 1:2–3). Poets and artists have discerned it all too well. Few caught this sentiment with greater poignancy than the nineteenth-century Romantic poet Percy Bysshe Shelley in his poem *Ozymandias*:

I met a traveller from an antique land
Who said: "Two vast and trunkless legs of stone
Stand in the desert. Near them on the sand,
Half sunk, a shattered visage lies, whose frown
And wrinkled lip and sneer of cold command
Tell that its sculptor well those passions read
Which yet survive, stamped on these lifeless things,
The hand that mocked them and the heart that fed.
And on the pedestal these words appear:
'My name is Ozymandias, King of Kings:
Look on my works, ye mighty, and despair!'
Nothing beside remains. Round the decay
Of that colossal wreck, boundless and bare,
The lone and level sands stretch far away."

Surely, you might say, this is too pessimistic a view of life. Do we not discern the beauty of a Mozart symphony, a painting by Rembrandt, or even this very poem by Shelley? These are works of beauty and grace, are they not?

Indeed they are, but the works themselves, no matter how beautiful, cannot erase the fact that their creators lie dead in their graves, their lives cut short (Shelley died at thirty). Death is the great leveller, and in the end, this world cannot produce what it might otherwise promise. There is a vanity, an emptiness, that some have discerned with crystal-clear vision. The world is cursed by God (Gen. 3:17–19).

Suffering under the curse

Life under the curse is marked by suffering. It is unavoidable. This is how Paul reasons: "We suffer with [Christ] *in order that* we may also be glorified with him" (Rom. 8:17, emphasis added). "In order that . . ." What do these words mean? Quite simply, there is no pathway to glory apart from the one that leads through testing and suffering. This is why John Calvin, commenting on 1 Peter 1:11, writes:

> The Church of Christ has been from the beginning so constituted, that the cross has been the way to victory, and death a passage to life. . . . The order is to be noticed; he mentions sufferings first, and then adds the glories which are to follow. For he intimates that this order cannot be changed or subverted; afflictions must precede glory. So there is to be understood a twofold truth in these words, — that Christians must suffer many troubles before they enjoy glory, — and that afflictions are not evils, because they have glory annexed to them.[46]

In light of this truth, Peter issues a pastoral word of advice about suffering: do not be *surprised* by it (1 Peter 4:12). But we often are. We complain about suffering, regard it as an unnecessary obstacle to usefulness, and question God's care because of it.

Listen to Peter again: glory comes on the other side of testing "so that the . . . genuineness of your faith — more precious than gold that perishes though it is tested by fire — may be found to result in praise and glory and honor at the revelation of Jesus Christ" (1 Peter 1:7).

All this may sound strange to twenty-first-century Christians in the Western world. In our entitlement culture, the "gospel" too often has been formulated in these terms: come to Jesus and all your troubles will disappear. Televangelists regularly proclaim "the best life now" as the essence of Christianity. The "name it and claim it, gab it and grab it" prosperity hucksters have conned too many into believing that suffering (poor health, poverty, rejection) have no place among those who truly love Jesus.

Union with Christ in suffering and glory

But what is a Christian, after all? He is one who is in union with Christ, who identifies with Jesus' *sufferings* as well as His glory (cf. Rom. 6:3–4). Significantly, when Paul expresses his longing to know the power of Christ's resurrection in his life, he understands all too well that it comes as he shares in Christ's sufferings (Phil. 3:10).

The link between suffering and glory is more than chronological—suffering *now*, glory *then*. The link is causal: we can see glory only through suffering. First comes affliction, through which we are brought to the end of ourselves and forced to lean on our Savior. Then comes glory.

Suffering does not always accomplish this goal. Of the two men who hung on crosses on either side of Jesus, suffering hardened one and humbled the other. When suffering accomplishes the latter, it is the pathway to heaven. Viewing it that way, we can understand how Peter can say, "Rejoice insofar as you share Christ's sufferings, that you may also rejoice and be glad when his glory is revealed" (1 Peter 4:13).

The "Futility" of the Planet

Not only do we suffer in this world, the world itself is suffering. Is it a mere coincidence that the Second Law of Thermodynamics (entropy) states that the universe is "running down"? Hardly. The Bible says so. The cosmos has been subjected to "futility" (Rom. 8:20).

How can the Jungfrau, the Matterhorn, the Grand Canyon, or Niagara Falls be subject to futility? These are among the great wonders of creation, and the sight of them takes our breath away. I have stood, for example, on the Jungfrau (at least, as far up as tourists may be taken by train), and the memory of it still evokes a sense of astonishment. But so long as man rather than God remains at center stage of creation, the world is subjected to futility. Not until sin is eradicated will creation yield the glory that God deserves.

From "futility" to freedom

As I write these lines, I am sitting in a hotel room in São Paulo, Brazil. Even here, just as in so many hotel rooms in the United States, my bathroom towel rail has a card that says, "Save the Planet." I am encouraged to reuse my wet towels in order to save the planet (and ensure greater profit for the hotel, of course).

The good news is that the planet will be saved—in a far more significant way than green politics can promise. Creation is going to be "born again." According to Paul, the universe is "groaning together in the pains of childbirth" (Rom. 8:22), anticipating what Jesus calls the "renewal of all things" (Matt. 19:28, NIV; Greek, *palingenesia*: *palin*, "again," and *genesis*, "beginning"). Earthquakes and tornadoes, hurricanes and droughts—these are not death pangs but birth pangs.

Presently, creation is:

» subject to "futility" (Rom. 8:20)
» groaning in the pains of childbirth (8:22)
» eagerly longing for the revealing of the sons of God (8:19)

But someday creation will:

» be set free from its bondage to corruption (8:21a)
» obtain the freedom of the glory of the children of God (8:21b)

A new world for new people

Both individual Christians (cf. John 3:3, 5) and the world itself are to be remade. The cosmos shares a future along with believers.

How could it be any other way? What environment, after all, could glorified believers—with new, resurrected bodies—occupy other than a physical one? It stands to reason that a *new world* must be created for us to dwell in.

In what sense will the world be "new"? Will it be altogether new, having no link with the old? No, it will be new in the sense of *re*newed. Both Peter and John speak of this new environment employing the Greek word *kainos* rather than *neos*, suggesting that the new universe stands in some measure of continuity with the present one (cf. 2 Peter 3:13; Rev. 21:1).[47]

Creation debates among Christians often stop short over issues relating to the age of the earth and the length of creation days. Sometimes, amid the maelstrom, we lose sight of the greater truth: God intends to create a "new heaven and new earth" (cf. Isa. 65:17; 66:22; 2 Peter 3:13).

God is going to regenerate creation. Paradise is to be restored.

The "Firstfruits" of the Spirit

Christians are "the firstfruits of the Spirit" (Rom. 8:23). We may experience suffering here and now, but a harvest is coming, the fruit of which will be perfect: "For I consider that the sufferings of this present time are not worth comparing with the glory that is to be revealed to us. . . . We ourselves, who have the firstfruits of the Spirit, groan inwardly as we wait eagerly for adoption as sons, the redemption of our bodies" (Rom. 8:18, 23).

The word translated "firstfruits" (Greek, *aparchē*) was also used to describe the birth certificate of a free man. The Spirit serves as our "birth certificate," testifying that we belong to the family of God and, more especially, that we belong to the Father.

The glory that is to come outweighs our suffering by a factor we cannot at present fathom, so much so that our present affliction by comparison with future glory appears "slight" and "momentary" (cf. 2 Cor. 4:17).

The Hebraic background to Paul's use of the word *glory* (Greek, *doxa*; Hebrew, *kabod*) signifies weight or heaviness. If we think of the way we sometimes employ the term *weighty* to mean "significant," we are close to what Paul has in mind. There is a profound weightiness to the glory that awaits believers. We are simply unable to grasp how great a blessing it will be: "No eye has seen, nor ear heard, nor the heart of man imagined, what God has prepared for those who love him" (1 Cor. 2:9, citing Isa. 64:4).

A firsthand experience of glory

The greater consolation is knowing that we will not simply observe the glory, that it will not merely be "revealed to us." Rather, we will experience it in a profoundly personal way, for we will be glorified. This is what Paul has in view when he speaks of "the redemption of our bodies."

No prayer of Jesus can ever be denied, and this is what He asked for in the hours before His death: "Father, I desire that they also, whom you have given me, may be with me where I am" (John 17:24a).

With Jesus.

Beholding His glory.

In the glory—*glorified*.

Take a moment and contemplate what is being said here. Your present sufferings may be excruciatingly painful. These trials you carry are cross-shaped (cf. Matt. 16:18). But they are a mere trifle in comparison with what God has in store for you. If we find that difficult to believe, it is because our view of glory is out of focus. Spiritual shortsightedness robs us of gospel comfort that God desires us to enjoy.

Mingling with splendors

Surely our vision of what lies before us is too small. *Great* things are in store for those who are in union with Jesus Christ.

Allow C. S. Lewis to expand your idea of what glorification is:

> We are to shine as the sun, we are to be given the Morning Star. I think I begin to see what it means. In one way, of course, God has given us the Morning Star already: you can go and enjoy the gift of many fine mornings if you get up early enough. What more, you may ask, do we want? Ah, but we want so much more—something the books on aesthetics take little notice of. But the poets and the mythologies know all about it. We do not want merely to *see* beauty, though, God knows, even that is bounty enough. We want something else which can hardly be put into words—to be united with the beauty we see, to pass into it, to receive it into ourselves, to bathe in it, to become part of it. That is why we have peopled air and earth and

water with gods and goddesses and nymphs and elves —
that, though we cannot, yet these projections can enjoy in
themselves that beauty, grace, and power of which Nature
is the image. That is why the poets tell us such lovely false-
hoods. They talk as if the west wind could really sweep into
a human soul; but it can't. They tell us that "beauty born
of murmuring sound" will pass into a human face; but it
won't. Or not yet. For if we take the imagery of Scripture
seriously, if we believe that God will one day *give* us the
Morning Star and cause us to *put on* the splendor of the
sun, then we may surmise that both the ancient myths and
the modern poetry, so false as history, may be very near the
truth as prophecy. At present we are on the outside of the
world, the wrong side of the door. We discern the freshness
and purity of morning, but they do not make us fresh and
pure. We cannot mingle with the splendours we see. But
all the leaves of the New Testament are rustling with the
rumors that it will not always be so. Some day, God willing, we shall get *in*. When human souls have become as
perfect in voluntary obedience as the inanimate creation
is in its lifeless obedience, then they will put on its glory,
or rather that greater glory of which Nature is only the first
sketch. . . . And in there, in beyond Nature, we shall eat of
the tree of life.[48]

What Paul describes is not the world we currently experience.
The world in which we live promises so much and sometimes — all

too often, in fact—we believe its lies. We are prone to succumb to its allurements, thinking that when we have them, we have something of great value. But the world decays all around us. What is new today is "used" tomorrow—try selling a new car you have just driven off the showroom floor.

Considering the world to come

How, then, should we view this world and our existence in it? The Puritans would answer, *sub specie aeternitatis*—"in the light of eternity": we must "consider" (Rom. 8:18) things as they will be rather than what they are now:

I see a world in decay and trouble.	I *consider* a renewed, perfect world to come.
I watch my body deteriorating.	I *consider* my new body.
I can make no sense of things here.	I *consider* a world where all is integrated.
I am tempted to sin here.	I *consider* a world of perfection to come.
I see in part now.	I *consider* a time when I shall see Jesus.

This is our calling: to gaze deliberately and see things as they *will be* rather than as they *are*.

Did you notice that Paul suggests that this deliberate gazing is what creation itself is doing? Creation "waits with eager longing," or, as J. B. Phillips so marvelously rendered it, "The whole creation is on tiptoe to see the wonderful sight of the sons of God coming into their own."[49]

Creation stands on tiptoe.

Are you?

ROMANS 8:26–27

"Likewise the Spirit helps us in our weakness.
For we do not know what to pray for as we ought,
but the Spirit himself intercedes for us
with groanings too deep for words.
And he who searches hearts
knows what is the mind of the Spirit,
because the Spirit intercedes for the saints
according to the will of God."

7

PRAYER POWER

(Romans 8:26–27)

" **J**ust as the first sign of life in an infant when born into the world, is the act of breathing," wrote J. C. Ryle, "so the first act of men and women when they are born again, is *praying*."[50] Every Christian prays. It is natural, necessary, and normal.

Prayer is one piece of the armor all Christians must put on each day to wage war against the world, the flesh, and the Devil (cf. Eph. 6:18). Jesus urged that Christians "ought always to pray and not lose heart" (Luke 18:1).

But prayer is not easy. Apart from making time for it, we often find that prayer *itself* is a struggle: our hearts are cold, our thoughts constantly wander, and our words descend into incoherent mumblings. Then, silence. The disciples fell asleep in Gethsemane despite being urged by Jesus to watchful prayer.

Donald Bloesch accurately and realistically titled his book on prayer *The Struggle of Prayer*.[51] As Robert Murray McCheyne is reputed to have said, if you want to humble a Christian, just ask about his or her prayer life. All of us who profess to be Christians acknowledge all too readily that in this area of our lives we feel a constant need for help.

As I write these lines, I am facing a difficult decision. I am trying to weigh my options, tallying pluses on one side and minuses on the other. I am trying to think clearly, rationally, and coherently, but it is a struggle. My decision will affect not only me but others: my family and my friends. What I want may not necessarily be what they want. And more importantly, what I want may not be what God wants. That is my problem: how can I know for sure what God wants for me? I have been saying to myself, "I wish God would just tell me what to do."

Most of us can relate to the perplexity that decision-making produces. And most of us can relate to the paralysis of prayer that often accompanies it. We wonder:

» Am I praying with an open mind?
» Am I weighing the options accurately?
» Am I forgetting an important piece of the equation?
» What *exactly* should I pray for?

Is there any help for us in this paralyzing weakness? Paul's answer is clear—yes, there is help. "The Spirit helps us in our weakness" (Rom. 8:26). Just as the "hope" (the *certainty*) of our future bodily redemption spurs us on amid the trials of this life (Rom. 8:24–25), so does the Spirit's assistance in prayer. God has not left us to fend for ourselves in our weakness.

Our Weaknesses in Prayer

At one level, prayer is an admission of weakness. We pray because we cannot meet a need ourselves. But prayer unveils for us the depth of our weakness, for not only are we unable to bring about what we ask for, we are not even capable of asking for the right things by our own strength: "We do not know what to pray for as we ought" (Rom. 8:26).

In fact, sometimes we cannot even put our requests into words. Have you found yourself unable to express your thoughts coherently in prayer? You find yourself reduced to groaning, a grown man or woman babbling like an infant. Evidently, Paul knew this experience, too. With all his massive intellect and Christian wisdom, he knew something of the sheer helplessness of indecision and uncertainty.

Seeking God's will in prayer

Some experience this helplessness when facing sickness—particularly when the sickness affects someone we love dearly. Ted Turner, the cable television mogul who provided funding for the movie *Gods and Generals*, gave an interview at the opening of the film in 2003. He reminded his interviewer that he had been brought up in a relatively strict Christian home. He even entertained the notion of becoming a missionary. But he had abandoned all that, and Christianity along with it. The reason? When his sister became very sick, he prayed for her recovery, but God did not answer his prayer. His sister died, so Turner dismissed Christianity.[52] He was embittered when he found that God's will was different from his will.

Bible folk struggled with God's will, too. When he was running away from Queen Jezebel, Elijah sat beneath the shade of a tree and prayed that God would take his life (1 Kings 19:4). Elijah could not see the big picture, the one that shows us the outcome of God's providence in our lives. He concluded that if he was going to die as Jezebel had threatened, he would rather have God take his life than for Jezebel to take credit for it.[53] Not knowing what else to ask of God, he prayed a prayer of utter hopelessness.

Paul, too, found himself uncertain of God's will. Three times he prayed for the removal of "a thorn" in the flesh (2 Cor. 12:8). But this was not God's will.

"Not as I will, but as you will"

More significantly, Jesus sensed that His human will was at odds with His Father's will. For that matter, His human will was at odds with His own divine will. He prayed, "My Father, if it be possible, let this cup pass from me; nevertheless, not as I will, but as you will" (Matt. 27:39). In His humanity, Jesus recoiled at what was being asked of the Servant. His human mind was not omniscient, so He had to calculate the cost of what was being required of Him based solely on the promises of God and the help of the Spirit. In Gethsemane, Jesus struggled in prayer with

His Father's will. He wanted His Father's will to be done; at the same time, He asked that another way might be revealed.

Earlier Jesus said, "I have come down from heaven, not to do my own will but the will of him who sent me" (John 6:38). He signaled not only a distinction between His will and His Father's will, but also the possibility that His natural preferences might not necessarily coincide with the wishes of the Father. Though Jesus remained sinless throughout His life, the fact that He struggled is surely sublime. It shows us, "We do not have a high priest who is unable to sympathize with our weaknesses" (Heb. 4:15).

Think about it: Jesus knew the struggle of prayer.

It was important to make the point above, but we need to add that there are struggles that come about in our prayer lives that are caused by sinful, rebellious tendencies within us—of which Jesus knew nothing.

The Spirit's Help in Prayer

The Spirit "helps" us to pray "in our weakness" (Rom. 8:26). The word Paul employs for "help" joins two prepositions to the main verb. Literally, it would be "with-for-help." The Spirit helps by praying with us *and* for us. In the Greek translation of the Old Testament, the word occurs in describing the way people were appointed to assist Moses "to bear the burden with [him]" (cf. Ex. 18:22; Num. 11:17). Also, the word is used in Luke when Martha requests that Jesus command her sister to join with her in helping (Luke 10:40).[54]

Several decades ago, the meaning of this word came to me

with some measure of clarity. I had been given a piano by a lady in the church who was "downsizing" in preparation for a move to a smaller apartment. The piano was very heavy and required a team of young deacons to help me move it to my house.

I vividly recall the attempt to carry the piano over the three or four steps through my front door. I had my hands firmly under a section of the piano, but can I honestly say I lifted that piano? The truth is, the young men were doing most of the lifting, even though I groaned along with them as this piano seemed to grow heavier with each step. So it is in prayer: we groan and, in so doing, we pray—however feeble the attempt. But the Holy Spirit prays "with" us, even "for" us, "with groans that words cannot express" (Rom. 8:26, NIV).

Our incoherent thoughts

We should put aside a longstanding interpretation from the time of John Chrysostom in fourth-century Constantinople. He viewed the groaning of which Paul writes as a reference to *glossolalia*, or tongues, a view that has been taken up in our time by Ernst Käsemann[55] and others. But as Sinclair Ferguson points out, "the element of heart-frustration and inexpressible emotion in what Paul says points us in another direction: incoherence. This is a portrayal of the absolute and total weakness of the believer, a weakness too weak to express his or her need coherently."[56] When all we can do is groan, the Spirit takes over.

But who exactly does the groaning—us or the Holy Spirit? Or is it both?

Commentators are divided. Some suggest that it is the Holy Spirit who groans, employing a language that we cannot fathom as He intercedes for us with our Father in heaven. Others are equally emphatic that the Spirit does *not* groan. It is *we* who groan, and the Spirit takes that groan and makes it into something coherent and intelligible. What emerges from within us (and sometimes it is an inaudible groan in the mind) is as unintelligible as the attempts at speech by those whose minds are impaired. But as I have discovered again and again, a mother always seems to understand what her child is saying and can vocalize it for the rest of us to understand without any difficulty, and God can do the same for His children.

The Spirit's eloquent intercession

When the Holy Spirit intercedes on our behalf, He speaks with divine eloquence. Carolyn Nystrom, who co-authored a book with J. I. Packer on prayer, put it this way: "The Spirit fixes our prayers on the way up."[57] Prayers that are badly expressed; prayers that are not really expressed at all; prayers that are just longings, aspirations, or groans—these prayers are "fixed" on their way up to our Father.

Consider the following scenario: You have unconverted children. You desire the Holy Spirit to come and regenerate them. You long for them to know and love Jesus. You find that they are in trouble. What are you going to pray for? Are you going to pray, "Lord, spare them the trouble?" What if it is God's way to humble them through affliction? Are you going to say, "Lord, bring trouble upon them if that is the way You are going to bring them to Yourself"?

In circumstances such as these, we often find ourselves "groaning," unsure of what to ask for in prayer. But God's certain promise to us is that Jesus' personal representative—the Holy Spirit—will come alongside us and help us in our praying.

What sweet comfort this promise gives us.

Our Reliance on God in Prayer

We are to "pray in the Holy Spirit" (Jude 20). We are not to pray in our own strength or with our own unaided insight. Praying in the Spirit involves reliance upon God, knowing that "if we ask anything according to his will he hears us" (1 John 5:14). We must pray with faith.

The Spirit also helps us pray from the heart. As Calvin writes, "And the Spirit is said to *intercede*, not because he really humbles himself to pray or to groan, but because he stirs up in our hearts those desires which we ought to entertain; and he also affects our hearts in such a way that these desires by their fervency penetrate into heaven itself."[58]

Can we know God's will with certainty? Paul's point is that it is not necessary for us to be certain. The Spirit knows the will of God. His presence with us provides us with reassurance that no matter how mixed-up we may be, He will overrule for us. With the Spirit's help, our prayers reach our Father in perfect form. The Holy Spirit's intercessions, like the intercessions of Jesus, are always heard, always answered.

What Paul speaks of here is what Jesus promised. When your faith is on trial, "do not be anxious about how you should defend yourself or what you should say, for the Holy Spirit will teach you in that very hour what you ought to say" (Luke 12:11–12).

This is the ministry the Spirit performs: He helps us when we are in need. He helps:

» a mother who sits beside a child's bed for days without sleep, too weak to cry for her offspring
» a spouse whose dreams of a happy marriage are destroyed by adultery and lies
» a breadwinner who has been laid off and can see no way of providing for the family

The Spirit helps.

The Spirit prays with us.

The Spirit's prayers are perfect because He knows the mind of God (Rom. 8:27).

God can never turn down a request from the Spirit.

Never.

ROMANS 8:28–30

"And we know that for those who love God
all things work together for good,
for those who are called according to his purpose.
For those whom he foreknew he also predestined
to be conformed to the image of his Son,
in order that he might be the firstborn
among many brothers.
And those whom he predestined he also called,
and those whom he called he also justified,
and those whom he justified he also glorified."

- 8 -

A GOLDEN CHAIN

(Romans 8:28–30)

If you live inside this massive promise, your life is more solid and stable than Mount Everest. Nothing can blow you over when you are inside the walls of Romans 8:28. Outside of Romans 8:28 all is confusion and anxiety and fear and uncertainty. Outside this promise of all-encompassing future grace there are straw houses of drugs and alcohol and numbing TV and dozens of futile diversions. There are slat walls and tin roofs of fragile investment strategies and fleeting insurance coverage and trivial retirement plans. There are cardboard fortifications of deadbolt locks and alarm systems and antiballistic missiles. Outside are a thousand substitutes for Romans 8:28.

91

Once you walk through the door of love into the massive unshakable structure of Romans 8:28 everything changes. There come into your life stability and depth and freedom. You simply can't be blown over anymore. The confidence that a sovereign God governs for your good all the pain and all the pleasure that you will ever experience is an incomparable refuge and security and hope and power in your life.[59]

So writes John Piper in his book, *Future Grace*. Outside Romans 8:28, there is only despair.

Paul has been reminding us about the complete adequacy of God to help us in every conceivable circumstance. The grace of God is adequate to meet:

» the guilt of sin (8:2–4)
» the downward drag of indwelling sin (8:5–13)
» the death and corruption of the world order that sin has brought about (8:16–23)
» the paralyzing inadequacy that we sometimes feel in prayer (8:26–27)

Now Paul makes a claim that covers every possible contingency. Nothing happens without God's total, meticulous, and unrelenting care and attention. In the words of the Westminster Shorter Catechism, "God's works of providence are, his most holy, wise, and powerful preserving and governing all his creatures, and all their actions."[60] His providence governs *everything*.

Assurance of God's Care

This bare statement of doctrine—the total providential control of God—can appear cold and impersonal, the stuff of theological discussion in comfortable armchairs. But consider this scenario:

As I write, my eye has caught sight of a framed picture that sits in my office. It is a picture of a young girl who suffers from a terrible brain malformation. She is now in her thirties, though the picture shows her when she was ten. From the moment of her birth, and the departure (within days) of her father, who could not face the prospect of raising her, her mother has cared for her with undying grace and devotion. As her daughter lives life in a minor key, her mother has found refuge in the assurance that the Lord is sovereign. His overruling providence explains the circumstance she now finds herself in, but it also gives her the resources by which she provides the love and tenderness that she shows each day.

The doctrine of providence for her is more than a mere statement of doctrine, abstract and detached; it is the daily source of assurance that there is meaning and purpose in what is otherwise cruel and senseless. So it should be for us.

Care for Christians

The assertion of providence in Romans 8:28 is specific and directed only to Christians. God rules over everything and everyone—believers and unbelievers—but his oversight is different in the case of believers. To them—and them *only*—

God's providence works "for good." The unwritten logical implication is that providence confirms the blessing of some and the doom of others. For those "who love God," providence is directed to achieve "good."

Who are "those who love God"? They are "those who are called according to [God's] purpose." The promise is given for those who are "called" by God into fellowship with Jesus Christ. Writing to the Corinthians, Paul addresses them as "the church of God that is in Corinth, . . . those sanctified in Christ Jesus, called to be saints" (1 Cor. 1:2). We could equally render the final phrase "called to be holy" or even "the holy called ones."[61] "Called ones" serves as a descriptive statement of what Christians are: they have experienced a sovereign call from the Lord, a calling that has brought them "out of darkness into his marvelous light" (1 Peter 2:9).

If you are not a believer, "a called one," this promise is not for you. You may not use this promise as a magic wand to provide yourself with assurance that everything will turn out fine in the end. Should you, for example, die in your condition of unbelief, providence has not been working for your good. "It is appointed for man to die once, and after that comes judgment" (Heb. 9:27).

However, for those who are Christians, Romans 8:28 encompasses their entire existence with divine assurance of watchful care and protection.

Care in "all things"

This is true for "all things," Paul writes, knowing that we will respond with questions like:

» What about bad things that happen to me that are not my fault?

» What about bad things that happen to me that are my fault?

» What about bad things that happen to others, whether my fault or not?

We can imagine the apostle saying, somewhat insistently: "Read the sentence again. What does it say? Does it not say, 'all things'? 'All' means *all*."

Paul is not suggesting that bad things will not happen to us. How could he possibly say such a thing when he writes so much about trials and tribulations that Christians are to expect? One of the very first lessons he learned during his first missionary journey was this one: "Through many tribulations we must enter the kingdom of God" (Acts 14:22). How could the one who wrote to the Galatians saying, "I bear on my body the marks of Jesus" (Gal. 6:17)—referring to the scars that crisscrossed his back from the thirty-nine lashes he received on five occasions (2 Cor. 11:24)—suggest anything different?

Many have been told that if they come to Jesus all their troubles will disappear, but it is not true. Christians are called to take up a cross and follow a crucified Savior. "If they persecuted me, they will also persecute you," Jesus warned (John 15:20).

Do bad things happen to God's people? Yes, they do. Disease, bankruptcy, divorce, and a thousand other evils occur in the lives of God's people. Some of the worst things I have seen occurred in the lives of the godliest Christians.

Why do such things happen? One response, heard all too frequently, is that God is not involved when bad things happen. God, it is said, stands aside and the bad things happen without His involvement. Satan did it. This fallen world did it. Fate did it. Nature did it.

But think about what this teaching is saying. It is asserting that there are circumstances in life over which God has no control. You may be driving along the highway when, suddenly, you cross into a "black hole" where God's providence has been withdrawn. You are on your own. You must face whatever evil is coming at you—a sudden urge to sleep, a drunken driver heading toward you, a deer caught in the headlights of your car, a mechanical fault that causes your car to veer off the road. If it is true that there are such black holes in which there can be no assurance of God's providential care, then there can be no assurance in God's love, no hope of security. It is a miserable, depressing thought.

There is none of this in Scripture. Bible characters believed in God's total providential care:

» Joseph was abandoned for dead, sold into slavery by his brothers, falsely accused of rape, and sentenced to serve his days in prison. But when circumstances changed and Joseph was the second-most-powerful man in Egypt, he said to his brothers, "You meant evil against me, but God meant it for good" (Gen. 50:20).

» Job was bereft of his ten children and his entire estate. But he uttered these memorable words: "The LORD gave, and the LORD has taken away; blessed be the name of the LORD" (Job 1:21). Again, when his health had been taken from him, he said to his wife, "Shall we receive good from God, and shall we not receive evil?" (Job 2:10).[62]

» Paul, speaking of his imprisonment in Rome, wrote to the Philippians, "I want you to know, brothers, that what has happened to me has really served to advance the gospel" (Phil. 1:12).

In order to maintain some semblance of human liberty, some insist that God does not govern the details, merely the big picture. But Romans 8:28 insists that God's providence governs the smallest, most incidental events, such as the death of sparrows and hair loss (cf. Matt. 10:29–31). Everything, in all its exquisite and intricate detail—things that others may consider trivial but are important to us—is governed by the overruling hand of God.

Care for a good end

"All things work together for *good*." But what exactly is the "good" that Paul has in mind? We might be tempted to think Paul is referring to philosophical discourses about the nature of "goodness," such as Plato discusses it in the *Republic*, where Socrates describes "the Form of the Good."[63] But that is not what Paul has in mind here. The text itself provides the explanation as to the "good" Paul has in view—conformity to the image of Jesus (Rom. 8:29). Providence is working to make us holy.

Holiness, as we have seen, is a work that begins at the moment of regeneration and ends when we are glorified in heaven. God is determined to make us like His Son, so He providentially determines that all things work toward this end.

If we are to become Jesus-like, there is a great deal of work for the Holy Spirit to do.

Assurance of God's Purpose

There is an order to the way in which the gospel comes to us and re-shapes us: "those whom he foreknew he also predestined. . . . And those whom he predestined he also called, and those whom he called he also justified, and those whom he justified he also glorified" (Rom. 8:29–30). Five golden links of a chain[64] are identified:

Foreknowledge → Predestination → Calling
→ Justification → Glorification

Not all identifiable links in the application of the gospel are mentioned here. Paul omits, for example, regeneration, faith, repentance, adoption, and sanctification. His point in this section of Romans 8 is not to provide us with a complete picture; he merely wishes to indicate God's invincible purpose. What God begins, He completes.

There is a logical and necessary order to the application of redemption in our lives. Justification, for example, does not come *before* calling. Though it is possible to talk about justification as something that God decrees in eternity, there remains an existential aspect to it. No one is in a right standing with God until he or she has been *called* into union and fellowship with Christ. Similarly, glorification—the *experience* of it—can come only *after* justification, not before.

God's act of foreknowledge

The first of the links is foreknowledge. What does *foreknowledge* mean? It is important not to jump to conclusions without looking carefully at what Paul says. He does not, for example, tell us that God foreknew *something* about those who are eventually glorified—some moral virtue that accounts for their glorification or, perhaps, their choice of Jesus Christ. Paul tells us that God foreknew *them*.

The knowledge in view is more than intellectual; it is embracive and relational. God foreknows in the Old Testament sense: He loved these individuals before they actually had existence.[65] We find ourselves trusting in Jesus Christ alone for salvation because God set His love on us in eternity. Our faith is not the ground of God's love. God's love—eternal love—is the ground of our faith.

God's act of predestination

Having set His love on us, God establishes our final destiny. He determines to save us and ensure that we will share fellowship with Him for eternity. He predestines us:

"He chose us in him before the foundation of the world." (Eph. 1:4)

"He predestined us for adoption." (Eph. 1:5)

"We have obtained an inheritance, having been predestined according to the purpose of him who works all things according to the counsel of his will." (Eph. 1:11)

Every Christian, even those opposed to predestination, acknowledges the truth of God's sovereignty by giving thanks to God for his or her salvation. Instead of patting themselves on the back for their intuitive insight and wisdom in choosing Jesus, they praise the Lord for their salvation. I have never heard any professing Christian say: "How clever of me to choose Jesus."

A sovereign determination accounts for our being Christians. Whatever philosophical objections we may have, we acknowledge with thankfulness the truth expressed so well in these lines:

Tis not that I did choose thee,
For, Lord, that could not be;
This heart would still refuse thee,
Hadst thou not chosen me.[66]

And these,

I sought the Lord, and afterward I knew.
He moved my soul to seek Him, seeking me;
It was not I that found, O Savior true;
No, I was found of Thee.[67]

Writing about election, John Calvin likened it to a family secret that only those who know God are able to appreciate:

> If it is plain that it comes to pass by God's bidding that salvation is freely offered to some while others are barred from access to it, at once great and difficult questions spring up, explicable only when reverent minds regard as settled what they may suitably hold concerning election and predestination. . . . They think nothing more inconsistent than that out of the common multitude of men some should be predestined to salvation, others to destruction. . . . We shall never be clearly persuaded, as we ought to be, that our salvation flows from the wellspring of God's free mercy until we come to know his eternal election.[68]

Those who refuse to bow to what God has revealed in His Word always cavil with the notion that a sovereign power governs all things. Only those who have learned the grace of submission can appreciate the beauty of divine sovereignty. We recognize its truth and respond in gratitude once we have experienced the grace of the gospel. God sets His love upon us and predestines us.

God's act of calling

He then calls us into fellowship and union with Christ. The outward form by which that call comes may be different—a sermon, a personal testimony by a friend, or (as in my own case) through reading a book.[69] But one way or another, every conversion is the result of God's calling. Without a call from God, we would not and could not believe in Jesus Christ. As we saw above, Christians are "called ones."

God's act of justification

The next word Paul employs is *justified*. We are called into union with Jesus Christ, and thereby we find ourselves in a right relationship with God. God judicially credits our sins to Jesus Christ, and credits Christ's righteousness to us. By faith, we receive all that Christ has done for us, propitiating God's wrath against sin by His sufferings on the cross on our behalf. Through an act of substitution, Jesus is reckoned sin and judged accordingly, and we are reckoned "the righteousness of God" in union with Christ and accepted into fellowship with God (cf. 2 Cor. 5:20–21).

Being "justified by faith we have peace with God" (Rom. 5:1).

God's act of glorification

God set His love on me. He chose me. He drew me with the cords of love. He justified me. What next? A life of onward and upward growth in grace—what the Bible calls holiness or "sanctification." However, Paul makes a beeline to "glorification."

But isn't glorification still future for us? Yes, but it is so certain that we will be glorified that Paul can speak of it as something that has already taken place. For, in part, it has. Christians are "raised . . . up" with Christ and are "seated . . . with him in the heavenly places" (Eph. 2:6). The glory that shall be revealed to us (Rom. 8:18) is spoken of here as a *fait accompli*.

God has an invincible purpose—to conform us to Jesus' likeness. To accomplish it, He may lead us through many trials and tribulations. But this one thing "we *know*" (Rom. 8:28, emphasis added): God will not abandon His grip on us. Rather, He will cause all things to work together for our good.

Glory awaits every child of God.

ROMANS 8:31–32

"What then shall we say to these things?
If God is for us, who can be against us?
He who did not spare his own Son
but gave him up for us all,
how will he not also with him
graciously give us all things?"

GOD FOR ME

(Romans 8:31–32)

G od is working everything for the ultimate good of those who love Him.

But do I love Him? Do I *really* love Him?

Am I "called according to his purpose" (Rom. 8:28b)?

Did God set His love on *me* in eternity?

Did God predestine *me* to believe in Jesus and share in the glory to come?

These are difficult questions, touching on our experience, which, frankly, vacillates. We ask ourselves these kinds of questions when all hell seems to break loose around us. When Satan shoots his fiery darts in my direction, and I feel their sting, how can I know that God still loves me? Does God still love me when I fail Him and let Him down by listening to the Devil?

Satan does seem to be in Paul's mind when he asks, "What

then shall we say to these things?" (v. 31a), because in expanding the question he immediately switches from "what" to "who" in a series of four interrogatives that follow:

» "*Who* can be against us?" (v. 31)
» "*Who* shall bring any charge against God's elect?" (v. 33)
» "*Who* is to condemn?" (v. 34)
» "*Who* shall separate us from the love of Christ?" (v. 35)

Clearly, "the accuser of our brothers" (Rev. 12:10) is in view. Satan desires nothing less than to dismantle the assurance that the gospel provides. And what better way to begin than to suggest that God is *against* us. "Take a good look at what is happening to you," Satan says. "How can you possibly believe that God loves you when these terrible events occur?"

John Bunyan writes in *The Pilgrim's Progress* of the way in which Satan (Apollyon) can make us afraid by painting a dark picture of what we can expect if we give ourselves to God:

Consider again when thou art in cool blood, what thou art like to meet with in the way that thou goest. Thou knowest that for the most part, his Servants come to an ill end, because they are transgressors against me and my ways: How many of them have been put to shameful deaths; and besides, thou countest his service better than mine whereas he never came yet from the place where he is to deliver any that served him out of our hands; but as for me, how many times, as all the World very well knows, have I delivered, either by power or fraud, those that have faithfully served me, from him and his.[70]

Serving God is costly, and Satan knows it. Serving Satan, at least from a this-worldly point of view, costs less. "Serve me," Satan says, "and you will never have to be afraid." This is a lie that too easily deceives us.

When David found himself seized by the Philistines in Gath, running as he was from the megalomaniac death threats of King Saul, he wrote in a psalm this word of assurance: "My enemies trample on me all day long, for many attack me proudly. When I am afraid, I put my trust in you. . . . This I know, that God is for *me*" (Ps. 56:2–3, 9, emphasis added).

God is *for* me. But how can I be certain?

The Love of the Father

Paul's first answer is that we should recall "these things" (v. 31a). But *what things*?

- » Those who are justified by faith alone are not condemned (Rom. 8:1).
- » God has sent His Son to condemn sin in the flesh (v. 3).
- » Those indwelt by God's Spirit may look forward to a bodily resurrection (vv. 12–14); indeed, present suffering is temporary and should be endured patiently (v. 25) and viewed as birth pangs anticipating our future bodily resurrection (v. 23).

» The Spirit witnesses with our spirits as to our adoption
and inheritance (vv. 16–17).

» We are surrounded by a comprehensive providence
that ensures the achievement of God's final purpose —
our conformity to the image of Christ (vv. 28–30).

Summarizing the entire chapter, Paul can now say: "If God
is for us, who can be against us? He who did not spare his own
Son but gave him up for us all, how will he not also with him
graciously give us all things?" (vv. 31b–32).

Our security is grounded in the objectivity of the finished
work of Jesus Christ on our behalf. But it is not, initially at least,
the love of Jesus that is in Paul's mind; it is the love of the Father
who sent Him. In this, Paul echoes John:

"For God so loved the world, that he gave his only Son."
(John 3:16)

"In this the love of God was made manifest among us, that
God sent his only Son into the world." (1 John 4:9)

The Puritan John Owen reflects on the importance of the
Father's love in the life of a Christian:

Assure yourself, there is nothing more acceptable unto the
Father than for us to keep up our hearts unto Him as the
eternal fountain of all that rich grace which flows out to
sinners in the blood of Jesus.

This will be exceeding effectual to endear your soul unto God, to cause you to delight in Him, and to make your abode with Him.

Many saints have no greater burden in their lives than that their hearts do not come clearly and fully up, constantly to delight and rejoice in God—that there is still an unwillingness of spirit unto close walking with Him. What is at the bottom of this distemper?

Is it not their unskillfulness in or neglect of this duty, even of holding communion with the Father in love? So much as we see of the love of God, so much shall we delight in Him, and no more. Every other discovery of God, without this, will but make the soul fly from Him.

But if the heart be once much taken up with this the eminency of the Father's love, it cannot choose but be overpowered, conquered, and endeared unto Him. This, if anything, will work upon us to make our abode with Him.

If the love of a father will not make a child delight in him, what will? Exercise your thoughts upon this very thing, the eternal, free, and fruitful love of the Father, and see if your hearts be not wrought upon to delight in Him.

I dare boldly say: believers will find it as thriving a course as ever they pitched on in their lives. Sit down a little at the fountain, and you will quickly have a further discovery of the sweetness of the streams.

You who have run from Him, will not be able, after a while, to keep at a distance for a moment.[71]

God is our Father by the Spirit of adoption; we now call Him "Abba! Father!" (Rom. 8:15). We have the inestimable privilege of employing the same name Jesus used when He said to Mary, "I am ascending to my Father and your Father, to my God and your God" (John 20:17).

Moreover, this Father loves us. This fact alone is worthy of contemplation. The thought of not being loved unhinges us. Therapeutic skills are required to help those who feel unloved and unwanted. But Christians know that they have been loved from eternity.

The Sacrifice of the Son

Paul's second answer to the question of how we can be sure God is for us is the cross. Biblical Christianity is cross-centered because it was at Calvary that the love of God for sinners like me was displayed in all its amazing fullness. On Calvary, in order to save us, the Father "did not spare" His Son, but "gave him up for us all" (Rom. 8:32a).

The language of "not sparing" points us to an interesting possibility. Was Paul thinking of the language found in the Greek translation of the Old Testament (the Septuagint, the preferred Bible translation of Paul's day)? God saw that Abraham was willing to not spare his son Isaac, but He commanded him not to kill the boy (Gen. 22:12). God spared Isaac, but He did *not* spare His own Son.

Similarly, the verb "gave" (or "delivered") is employed in the Gospels (especially Matthew) to describe what happened to Jesus:

» "The Son of Man will be *delivered* over to the chief priests and scribes" (Matt. 20:18, emphasis added).

» "What will you give me if I *deliver* him over to you?" (Matt. 26:15, Judas speaking to the chief priests, emphasis added).

» "When morning came, all the chief priests and the elders of the people took counsel against Jesus to put him to death. And they bound him and led him away and *delivered* him over to Pilate the governor" (Matt. 27:1–2, emphasis added).

» "Pilate said to them, 'Whom do you want me to release for you: Barabbas, or Jesus who is called Christ?' For he knew that it was out of envy that they had *delivered* him up" (Matt. 27:17–18, emphasis added).

» "Then he released for them Barabbas, and having scourged Jesus, *delivered* him to be crucified" (Matt. 27:26, emphasis added).[72]

The idea of "not sparing" lies at the heart of the hymn "How Great Thou Art":

And when I think that God, His Son not sparing,
Sent Him to die, I scarce can take it in;
That on the cross, my burden gladly bearing,
He bled and died to take away my sin.[73]

"Who killed Jesus? Who killed Him?" Octavius Winslow asks. "It wasn't Judas out of greed. It wasn't the Jews out of envy. It was

His Father out of love. The Father killed Him. It was the Father who put Him to death."[74]

God the Father did not spare Him *for our sakes*.

Jesus asked the Father to spare Him

That the Father did not spare His own Son the pains of Calvary is all the more startling given the fact that Jesus *asked to be spared*. In Gethsemane, He cried, "My Father, if it be possible, let this cup pass from me" (Matt. 26:39). Jesus was asking to be spared Calvary. True, He went on to yield Himself to His Father's will ("Not as I will, but as you will"), but this should not diminish the urgency and focus of the request. In the anguish of Jesus' soul, His sweat fell to the ground like drops of blood (Luke 22:44). He prayed "with loud cries and tears" (Heb. 5:7). "No one ever feared death so much as this man," wrote Martin Luther.[75] In this prayer, Jesus' entire soul and body were focused on one thing: to be spared the trial that awaited Him.

This was no ordinary trial and no ordinary death. This was to be a death *with a sting*—a death that would lead Jesus to experience the torment of the wicked damned. And He had to face it without atonement for the sin reckoned to Him.

The wonder of Calvary is not only the love of the heavenly Father that it displays; it is the love of the Son in His compliance with the Father's will despite the unimaginable horror of what it would cost Him. "Greater love has no one than this, that someone lays down his life for his friends. You are my friends . . ." (John 15:13–14a).

The Father could not spare Jesus

Calvary takes on an even greater mystery: the Father *could not* spare Him. The Scriptures disclose that deep in eternity, before the creation of the world and the entrance of sin, God—Father, Son and Holy Spirit—conceived a plan to save sinners. Whatever we call this plan—historically it has been called the *pactum salutis*, or covenant of redemption—the arrangements of divine wisdom and love on the part of the three persons of the Godhead set out to save sinners—to save *me*.

The Father *could not* spare His Son, but what was clear to the divine mind and will of Jesus was, for a moment, veiled to His human mind and will. It is all the more poignant, therefore, that in the darkness of Gethsemane, Jesus yielded in total and perfect submission to the will of His Father. Without the aid of a voice saying, "I love you"—a voice that He heard at His baptism and on the Mount of Transfiguration (Matt. 3:17; 17:5)—Jesus had to *believe* that His Father loved Him. He had to trust His Father's love for Him even when the circumstances pointed to the contrary. In the darkness, Jesus had to *believe* that a light was shining that He could not see.

In his book *Lament for a Son*, philosopher-theologian Nicholas Wolterstorff writes of the tragic death of his son in a climbing accident. In a preface to the book, he writes: "If someone asks, 'Who are you, tell me about yourself,' I say—not immediately, but shortly—'I am one who lost a son.' That loss determines my identity; not all my identity, but much of it. It belongs within my story."[76]

Our heavenly Father is defined by the fact that He, too, is One who has lost a Son—handed over *to* sinners *for* sinners. When we look at the cross, it almost seems as though the Father loves us *more* than He loves His own Son. That cannot be, of course, but it looks like that. He loves us that much. No greater evidence of the Father's love for us is imaginable or necessary.

The Provision of "All Things"

Paul's conclusion is simple: "How will he not also with him graciously give us all things?" (Rom. 8:32b). The love of the Father expressed in the sacrifice of the Son achieves "all things" for those God loves. Here is the final evidence that God is for us.

What exactly does the phrase "all things" mean? The answer lies in the previous verses: God in His providence is working "all things" together in order to achieve a specific goal—our glorification (Rom. 8:28, 30). Everything that happens to us is designed to ensure that God's plan—foreknowledge-predestination-calling-justification-glorification—is brought about. "All things" refers to the final, complete fruition of our redemption in glory.

The gospel guarantees that we will be brought home to glory. It is by grace that we are saved from the consequences of our sin; the same grace of God in the gospel brings us home. Better, *Jesus* brings us home. Our salvation is bound up not in something intangible and impersonal, but in a person—in Jesus Christ. The grace that ensures our final glorification is the grace of God in Jesus Christ.

The gospel—the *good news* (Greek, *euangelion*)—is that God has provided for sinners like me a *Substitute*, One who takes my place and bears the consequences of my sin. At the cross, the wrath that my sins deserve was poured out on the Substitute. Justice was satisfied and atonement was given. My sins were imputed to the Substitute; His righteousness (obedience) was imputed to my account. I received the benefits of the cross by faith *alone*.

Who is the Substitute? He is Jesus, my Savior.

Because Paul saw the cross as central to the gospel, he could say, "We preach Christ crucified" (1 Cor. 1:23). And again, "I decided to know nothing among you except Jesus Christ and him crucified" (1 Cor. 2:2). And again, "I delivered to you as of first importance what I also received: that Christ died for our sins in accordance with the Scriptures" (1 Cor. 15:3). The cross was of "*first* importance." To cite Greg Gilbert:

> Scripture makes it clear that the cross *must* remain at the center of the gospel. We cannot move it to the side, and we cannot replace it with any other truth as the heart, center, and fountainhead of the good news. To do so is to present the world with something that is not saving, and that is therefore not good news at all.[77]

Is the cross *that* central in your life?

ROMANS 8:33–34

"Who shall bring any charge against God's elect?
It is God who justifies. Who is to condemn?
Christ Jesus is the one who died—more than that,
who was raised—who is at the right hand of God,
who indeed is interceding for us."

- 10 -

FACING
THE ACCUSER

(Romans 8:33–34)

In the classic allegory *The Pilgrim's Progress*, when John Bunyan describes Christian's encounter with Apollyon (i.e., Satan), he touches on something that every believer knows all too well. Satan insinuates (and he is a master in the art of insinuation) that, for all Christian's devotion and zeal, he has nevertheless been unfaithful. Christian has failed to keep up his promise of unswerving discipleship.

Failure. It cripples us and drains us of energy. We desire to give ourselves to God, but every day brings evidence of failure. Broken promises. Flagging zeal. And sins—too many of them, red and raw. How can we be such failures in the light of the gospel?

Satan loves to point out our hypocrisy. It is one of his favorite weapons.

Bunyan knew this charge well, so into Christian's mouth he places the following reply to Apollyon: "All this is true, and much more which you have left out; but the Prince whom I serve and honour is merciful and ready to forgive. Besides, these sins possessed me in your own country; I have groaned under them, been sorry for them, but now have obtained pardon from my Prince."[78]

Christian's response is more than insightful; it is pastoral and gospel-focused, demonstrating Bunyan's acquaintance with the grammar of the gospel. The way to deal with satanic accusations of inconsistency and guilt is to say: "It's worse than you think. If my salvation depends on my consistency, I am lost. But it doesn't. My past, present, and future sins are covered by the blood of Jesus."

The only firm ground

My good works can never be the *ground* of my acceptance with God—not at the point of conversion or at any subsequent point in Christian advancement. Let Satan hurl all the charges he dare—the basis of my acceptance with God stands firm and secure. I am justified on the basis of the finished work of Jesus Christ *alone*, today as much as on any day to come.

C. H. Spurgeon wrote:

Christ did not love you for your good works. They were not the cause of His beginning to love you. So, He does not love you for your good works even now. They are not the cause of His continuing to love you. He loves you because He loves you.[79]

God loves you because He loves you. So stop trying to add, "Yes, but the real reason He loves me is because of my good works."

The ploys of the accuser

Satan is "the accuser of our brothers" (Rev. 12:10). As we saw in the previous chapter, in asking a series of "who" rather than "what" questions, Paul is thinking about Satan's ploys in attacking us:

>> "*Who* can be against us?" (Rom. 8:31b)
>> "*Who* shall bring any charge against God's elect?" (v. 33)
>> "*Who* is he who condemns?" (v. 34a)
>> "*Who* shall separate us from the love of Christ?" (v. 35a)

All of these ploys, real or hypothetical, have one thing in common: they are designed to unsettle the believer and rob him or her of assurance and peace in the gospel.

In a recent book titled *By Grace Alone*, Sinclair Ferguson helpfully labels these four ploys "Satan's 'fiery darts.'"[80] He summarizes them in this way:

>> Fiery Dart 1: "God is against you," Satan says. "He is not really for you. How can you believe He is for you when you see the things that are happening in your life?"

» Fiery Dart 2: "I have accusations I will bring against you because of your sins," Satan argues. "What can you say in your defense? Nothing."

» Fiery Dart 3: "You say you are forgiven, but there is a payback day coming—a condemnation day," Satan insinuates. "How will you defend yourself then?"

» Fiery Dart 4: "Given your track record, what hope is there that you will persevere to the end?" Satan asks.[81]

Let us look more closely at these satanic ploys. We will consider the first three in the remainder of this chapter, then think through the fourth in the next chapter.

"God Cannot Be Trusted"

"Who can be against us?" (Rom. 8:31b).

Satan insinuates that God is against us. This is an attack on the character of God. When bad things happen to us, when our plans are constantly frustrated, Satan suggests, "God is against you." We tend to believe him.

This is a well-used weapon in Satan's armory. He first used it in Eden, suggesting that God had forbidden Adam and Eve access to the tree "in the midst of the garden" (Gen. 3:3) because God didn't really love them.

Satan's attempt to sow distrust began with the *form* in which his initial question was put: "Did God actually say, 'You shall not eat of any tree in the garden'?" (Gen. 3:1). God had said no such thing, of course, and Satan knew that. But that didn't stop him from

120

making the suggestion that there was something ungenerous, even suspicious, about the provision God had made for Adam and Eve. God's character, the Devil insinuated, was loving only *to a degree*. Behind the façade lay a darker truth: God was depriving Adam and Eve of something necessary to the full enjoyment of life.

God cannot be trusted, Satan suggested in the garden. He continues to insinuate this thought today. Satan says that God is *for* me one day and *against* me the next. God is fickle.

The answer to this charge, as we saw earlier, lies *extra nos* ("outside ourselves"), as Martin Luther said. We must look to Jesus Christ and what He has done for us, not at ourselves or our experiences. God's love is not, like our emotions, a vacillating thing, here one day and gone the next.

Only a cross-centered theology can undo the suspicion aroused by Satan's first charge. In the light of the cross, I can say no less than "He loves me with an infinite love." God gave up His Son for me. There can be no greater demonstration of His love.

"You Are a Wretched Sinner"

"Who shall bring any charge against God's elect?" (Rom. 8:33).

Satan's second ploy is aimed at our feeble discipleship. We keep on sinning despite our best endeavors. We keep on failing.

We sometimes respond to the constant failures of others by saying: "I've had enough. I can take no more." Thus, we are prone to think that God responds this way, that He looks on His children and says: "Look at you! You keep failing, and I've had enough."

To an extent, this scenario is true. The Bible does seem to

121

indicate that there is a limit to God's patience. The book of Amos, for example, contains a repeated phrase: "For three transgressions . . . and for four" (Amos 1:3, 6, 9, 11, 13; 2:1, 4, 6). God did not chastise His people for the first or even the second transgression. He was patient with them. But there come times when God's patience runs out—after "three" and "four" transgressions.

The Bible warns us about God's discipline. And yet, according to the book of Hebrews, discipline is evidence of God's love for us: "My son, do not regard lightly the discipline of the Lord, nor be weary when reproved by him. For the Lord disciplines the one he loves, and chastises every son whom he receives. . . . God is treating you as sons" (Heb. 12:5–7).

Jeopardizing our adoption?

When Paul says, "Who shall bring any charge against God's elect?" he does not intend to deny God's work of discipline in our lives. But the charge that Satan makes is more than that; he insinuates that our failures imply that we are no longer adopted children.

There is a subtlety here that may elude us: Satan is suggesting that unless we maintain a certain level of productivity, our status as adopted sons is in jeopardy. God loves me when my zeal is at a certain level, but He doesn't love me quite so much when my sin abounds. In order to sustain God's love, I need to maintain a level of sanctification.

This is reminiscent of a marriage that has grown sour. Mistrust abounds, and one spouse is desperately trying to do something to win back the affection of the other. But is this how God relates to us in the gospel? Is God's love really as fitful as Satan wants us to

122

think? Like the elder brother in Jesus' parable, have we begun to think that our service is in fact a form of slavery (Luke 15:29)?

Relying on Jesus' finished work

What is Paul's response? "It is God who justifies" (Rom. 8:33). The answer to Satan's accusations of ongoing failure is to return to the basis on which God accepts us in the first place: our justification. Paul runs to the gospel and the finished work of Christ.

This is what David Dickson (1583–1662) did. In December 1662, he became extremely sick. When a friend asked him what he was thinking, he wisely said, "I have taken all my good deeds, and all my bad deeds, and have cast them together in a heap before the Lord, and have fled from both to Jesus Christ, and in Him I have sweet peace."[82]

Our initial acceptance—our right standing with God—is based entirely on the free grace God offers to needy and hopeless sinners in Jesus Christ. God pronounces that sinners like us are, in fact, righteous—as righteous as Jesus is. How? By crediting our sins to His Son and His Son's righteousness to us (cf. 2 Cor. 5:20–21). In achieving this status, we add nothing—not even the faith by which we receive it and claim it as ours. Faith, the Bible spells out clearly, is "the gift of God" (Eph. 2:8).

In bringing us back to our justification as the ground of our initial acceptance with God, Paul is saying in effect: the basis of God's love for you and acceptance of you has never depended on your good works—not at the point of entry and not now as you see yourself failing. It is no wonder John Calvin could write that justification is "the hinge on which the whole door of salvation swings."[83] Satan's accusations based on our failure should fall on deaf ears.

God's love is not dependent on the quality of our sanctification—if that were so, He would never have sent His Son for us. He would have spared Him.

"You Will Not Escape Your Guilt"

"Who is to condemn?" (Rom. 8:34a). Answer: "There is therefore now no condemnation for those who are in Christ Jesus" (Rom. 8:1).

Satan's accusations regarding our sins are met with simple statements (v. 34b):

- » Christ died.
- » Christ rose again.
- » Christ sits at God's right hand.
- » Christ intercedes on our behalf.

Jesus died

John Newton followed Paul's advice in one of his great hymns. He recounted his own experience as a Christian, of being bowed down beneath his sins and sorely pressed by Satan. Then he wrote:

I may my fierce accuser face, and tell him . . .

Tell him what exactly? Did he say: "I'm trying to live a better Christian life"? "I may have failed this week, but wait until you

124

see what I will do for Jesus next week"? "I will resolve to spend more time in prayer and Bible study"? Or perhaps, "I was saved on such and such a date"?

Such answers are tawdry, and Satan knows all too well how to turn them back on us for our destruction. Instead, Newton shows us the proper way to respond when the Devil comes against us with his accusations of failure:

I may my fierce accuser face, and tell him thou hast died.[84]

The same truth is contained in the contemporary song "In Christ Alone":

In Christ alone, who took on flesh,
Fullness of God in helpless babe;
This gift of love and righteousness,
Scorned by the ones He came to save.

'Til on that cross as Jesus died,
The wrath of God was satisfied;
For every sin on Him was laid,
Here in the death of Christ I live.[85]

On the cross, Christ atoned for all the sins of all God's elect. That includes *every* sin, including the sins that Satan's accusing tongue is now hurling against me. Jesus has borne the wrath and the Father has been satisfied. Justice has been done. My sins can never be brought against me as a charge ever again.

Augustus Toplady put it this way:

Payment God cannot twice demand—
First at my bleeding Surety's hand,
And then again at mine.[86]

Do you understand what Toplady is saying? My sin—all of it: past, present, and future—has been atoned for in the death of Christ. The debt owed to sin has been fully paid. The wrath that every one of my sins deserves has been poured out on Jesus as my substitute and sin-bearer. These sins *cannot* be punished again; not now, not tomorrow, not next week, not on the day of judgment. To do so would be double jeopardy. "Payment God cannot twice demand—first at my bleeding Surety's hand, and then again at mine."

Jesus rose again

In His resurrection, Jesus' righteousness was vindicated. The Father demonstrated His approval of His Son's accomplishment on the cross. The resurrection was the Father saying, "Well done, good and faithful servant."

Jesus sits at God's right hand

Jesus now sits at God's right hand in heaven. This is a regal picture of one who is resting in triumph. He sits on a throne because He is King and has conquered death, hell, and Satan. He sits because His atoning work is finished—"It is finished," He cried from the cross (John 19:30).

Jesus intercedes on our behalf

As He sits at God's right hand, Jesus intercedes for His people. His prayers for us can be heard by His (and our) Father. Several verses earlier, we were told of the Spirit's intercession for us (Rom. 8:27). Now we are told of the Son's intercession as well. We have two intercessors, two *divine* persons interceding on our behalf. Just think about it: Satan versus Jesus and the Holy Spirit. It is not a contest that Satan can win.

What does Jesus say to the Father? Perhaps something like this: "This one whom Satan is accusing is Mine. You gave him to Me before the foundation of the world. He's Mine. I died for him. I shed My blood for this one. I bore the wrath for him. I did it all—everything. Now, Father, help him in his struggles. Send the Holy Spirit to encourage him. Give him victory over his sins. Remind him of what I have done and give him peace."

Or, more particularly, like this:

"Father, I desire that they also, whom you have given me, may be with me where I am, to see my glory that you have given me because you loved me before the foundation of the world." (John 17:24)

Just a few years after my ordination to the ministry, an elderly lady told me something that I've never forgotten. At a point when I felt thoroughly dejected with my ministry, she said to me, "See no one in the picture but Jesus."

She was correct.

Jesus is all the approval we need.

ROMANS 8:35–39

"Who shall separate us from the love of Christ?
Shall tribulation, or distress, or persecution,
or famine, or nakedness, or danger, or sword?
As it is written, 'For your sake we are being
killed all the day long;
we are regarded as sheep to be slaughtered.'
No, in all these things we are more than
conquerors through him who loved us.
For I am sure that neither death nor life,
nor angels nor rulers, nor things present
nor things to come, nor powers,
nor height nor depth,
nor anything else in all creation,
will be able to separate us from the love of God
in Christ Jesus our Lord."

UNION WITH CHRIST— FOREVER

(Romans 8:35–39)

" He is no fool, to give what he cannot keep in order to gain what he cannot lose."[87] Jim Elliot wrote these words in his journal on October 28, 1949. Just over six years later, at the age of twenty-eight, he was murdered by Huaorani warriors on the Curaray River in Ecuador.

Elliot was sure that salvation cannot be lost. Nothing can separate us from the love of God in Jesus Christ. It is this assurance that lies at the heart of the peroration of Romans 8:

"For I am sure that neither death nor life, nor angels nor rulers, nor things present nor things to come, nor powers, nor height nor depth, nor anything else in all creation, will be able to separate us from the love of God in Christ Jesus our Lord." (Rom. 8:38–39)

So far, Paul has asked three questions pointing to three ploys of Satan:

» "Who can be against us?" (v. 31b)
» "Who shall bring any charge against God's elect?" (v. 33)
» "Who is he who condemns?" (v. 34a)

A fourth question is now asked:

» "Who shall separate us from the love of Christ?" (v. 35a)

Satan (the personal interrogative "Who" refers to him) again insinuates that what may be true of us today can be lost tomorrow. If it were dependent on our feeble efforts and resolve, he surely would be correct. But it is not: our salvation, from beginning to end, is God's work, and "he who began a good work in [us] will bring it to completion" (Phil. 1:6b).

Complete security

The theme that Paul now reflects upon is our complete security: no *one* and no*thing* can sever us from the arms of God's embrace. Peter reflected on it, too, affirming that Christians have an "inheritance that is imperishable, undefiled, and unfading, kept in heaven" (1 Peter 1:4).

How can we be sure of God's keeping? Because He loves us—a love, as J. I. Packer writes in *Knowing God*, that "is a function of omnipotence, and has at its heart an almighty purpose to bless which cannot be thwarted."[88]

God's love, then, is wedded to sovereign power and sovereign will. We say, "Where there's a will, there's a way," and when the will in question is God's, the way is certain. God wills to save us, to bring us home, and nothing can stop Him.

Strength in the face of death

The firm assurance of heaven to come—assurance of God's keeping power—keeps Christians strong when facing death.

Paul has already spoken in this chapter of life issuing from death. The whole creation, he has said, is going to be liberated from its bondage to decay (Rom. 8:18–25). A new heaven and new earth lie before us, what Jesus called a "regeneration" (Greek, *palingenesia*, Matt. 19:28). Our bodies will be resurrected and the cosmos will be regenerated. For this reason, tombs in old cemeteries often bear the inscription *mors janua vitae*—"death is the gateway to life."

When the Covenanter Walter Smith climbed the ladder to the scaffold and death, he turned to say goodbye to his relations and friends. Then he said: "Farewell all created enjoyments, pleasures and delights; farewell, sinning and suffering; farewell praying and believing, and welcome heaven and singing.

131

Welcome, joy in the Holy Ghost; welcome, Father, Son and Holy Ghost; into thy hands I commend my spirit."[89]

Every Christian may know that the day of his death is going to be his best day.

Beloved Children

When Paul asks, "Who shall separate us from the love of Christ?" whose love does he have in mind—our love for Christ or Christ's love for us? Some have argued the former, but it can only be the love of Christ for us.[90] Let me make this perfectly clear: if Paul is asking, "Who can separate me from *my* love for Jesus?" the answer is, "almost anything." If I am dependent on the upkeep and quality of my love for the Savior, there is no comfort in this passage of Scripture. My love is weak and faint. It fluctuates with the passing of days. The very threat of pain, loss, or hardship undoes my resolve. Is this not so with you?

Paul references *two* sources of love in these closing verses: the love of Jesus (vv. 35, 37) *and* the love of the Father (v. 39).

The gospel is especially welcome to individuals who have never been told that they are loved. The lack of genuine affection twists some out of shape. They are distrustful of affection when it is given, fearful that it is disingenuous and fleeting. To such insecurity, the gospel demonstrates a love that is immeasurable and eternal. The love of the Father and the Son in the gospel refuses to let us go:

> O Love that wilt not let me go,
> I rest my weary soul in thee . . .[91]

Nothing will separate Spirit-indwelt Christians from the love of the Father and the Son. God loved us when we were at our worst. He loved us when we were sinners in union with Adam:

"God shows his love for us in that while we were still sinners, Christ died for us." (Rom. 5:8)

God "did not spare his own Son but gave him up for us all." (Rom. 8:32)

The proof that we are loved as Christians is not found within ourselves, but at the cross. Calvary was the greatest demonstration of love the world has seen, because it was an act of selfless love in substitution:

What wondrous love is this, O my soul, O my soul!
What wondrous love is this, O my soul!
What wondrous love is this that caused the Lord of bliss
To bear the dreadful curse for my soul, for my soul,
To bear the dreadful curse for my soul![92]

Suffering Conquerors

What are the possible forces that seem to threaten to undo us and sever us from the love of God in the gospel? Paul lists seven items.

The list opens with tribulation (Greek, *thlipsis*), distress (Greek, *stenochōria*), and persecution (Greek, *diōgmos*). Taken together, they represent the external pressures brought about by a hostile world. Next come famine and nakedness, the lack of adequate food and clothing. Since Jesus promised in the Sermon on the Mount that food and clothing are basic commodities that God provides for His children, the absence of them might suggest all too easily that God does not care about us. Finally, Paul mentions danger and sword—the risk of death and the experience of it.

Much unrealism abounds in our time concerning suffering and the Christian life. Pain unsettles us more than it ought. Too often we think that belonging to Jesus frees us from the experience of pain and displeasure. Health-and-wealth hucksters fool too many into believing that life in the kingdom of God brings material and physical blessings that elevate us above the rest of society. Nothing is farther from the truth. Every page of the Gospel accounts of Jesus' life and ministry abound with warnings that trouble will dog the Christian every step of the way to heaven.

The seventeenth-century Puritan John Geree, writing on "The Character of an Old English Puritane or Non-Comformist (1646)," described not only the Puritan life but the Christian life: "His whole life he accounted a warfare, wherein Christ was his captain, his arms, praiers and tears. The Crosse his Banner and his word *Vincit qui patitur* [he who suffers conquers]."[93]

Likewise, Paul summed up the Christian life in this world in a short sentence: "I die every day" (1 Cor. 15:31).

Suffering is to be expected insofar as the saying is true: the closer we are to the King, the more likely we are to become targets of the enemy. Loyalty to Jesus will bring suffering as a matter of course: "As it is written, 'For your sake we are being killed all the day long; we are regarded as sheep to be slaughtered'" (v. 36; Ps. 44:22).

A certain salvation

And yet, in all of these sufferings "we are more than conquerors [Greek, *hypernikōmen*] through him who loved us" (Rom. 8:37). The cross guarantees the outcome of that which it achieved. And what did it achieve? Not the mere possibility of our salvation, but the certainty of it. The blood spilled in atonement propitiates the wrath sin deserves. Sin's penalty was paid in full. *Nothing* remains to hinder our salvation—no claim of Satan, no power of hell, no recalcitrant force in an untamed universe.

Paul speaks of his conviction—"I am sure"[94] (v. 38). Sure of what? In addition to the seven items he has already mentioned, he now names another ten forces that fail to sever us from Christ: death and life; angels and rulers; things present and things to come; powers; height and depth; and anything else in all creation (vv. 38–39).

The forces arrayed against us may be real or imaginary, present or future, actual or potential, definite or unspecified (e.g., anything else in all creation). The point is that *nothing* possesses the ability to sever us from the love of God in the gospel:

> The work which His goodness began,
> The arm of His strength will complete;
> His promise is Yea and Amen,
> And never was forfeited yet.

Things future, nor things that are now,
Nor all things below or above,
Can make Him His purpose forgo,
Or sever my soul from His love.

My name from the palms of His hands
Eternity will not erase;
Impressed on His heart it remains,
In marks of indelible grace.
Yes, I to the end shall endure,
As sure as the earnest is giv'n;
More happy, but not more secure,
The glorified spirits in heav'n.[95]

Gospel certainty

Only the gospel can provide the kind of assurance that we see in Paul's words at the close of Romans 8. Because our salvation comes *extra nos*, "from outside us" (to cite Martin Luther again), all our certainty in final perseverance lies in God's power and determination to save us. In the last analysis, our salvation does not depend on ourselves but on God's keeping power.

Were we to seek assurance through a sacramental treadmill of personal obedience, we could entertain no lasting certainty of our salvation. Cardinal Robert Bellarmine (1542–1621), from his Roman Catholic point of view, was absolutely correct in viewing the doctrine of assurance as the greatest of all Protestant heresies. If, as the Roman Catholic Church teaches, our final justification on the day of judgment is dependent on something we do in this life, there can be no assurance. But this is not where Paul wants us to be. Paul, along with the whole New Testament, desires us to be "sure" of salvation—now and forever.

The application of the gospel to sinners by the Holy Spirit (*ordo salutis*) guarantees everything, including perseverance. The justified saints will be brought home to glory—all of them.

Persevering Pilgrims

From "no condemnation" (v. 1) to "no separation" (v. 39), Paul has expounded for us the implications of justification by faith alone in Christ alone. But a caveat needs to be mentioned. Is it true that all who profess to be Christians will persevere? Reading Romans 8, we might respond to this question with a resounding "Yes." But that would be incorrect. It would, in fact, seriously misread the warning of the New Testament: "Take care, brothers, lest there be in any of you an evil, unbelieving heart, leading you to fall away from the living God" (Heb. 3:12). The warning of apostasy in this verse is more than hypothetical: if we fail to persevere, we *will* become apostate.

Two things need underlining as we look back over Paul's teaching in Romans 8. First, what is said about the certainty of future perseverance in this chapter is true of those who have been "foreknown" and "predestined" (v. 29). It is the elect, and *only* the elect, who make it all the way home.

Second, it is possible for people to think and say that they are Christians when they are not. These individuals may pass as Christians among their friends and be considered as such by the church—even a Bible-believing, gospel-centered, Christ-exalting church. In this respect, Christians—perhaps we should write "Christians"—can and do fall away. They are not "true Christians" for they are not regenerate and justified. They merely think they are, and other "true Christians" think so, too.

None of the disciples, for example, seemed to doubt the discipleship of Judas (though the Gospel authors, writing *after* the fact, inserted parenthetical explanations that Judas was the one who betrayed Jesus; Matt. 10:4; Mark 3:19; John 6:71). It is from this point of view that Paul could write, "For Demas, in love with this present world, has deserted me and gone" (2 Tim. 4:10).[96] More to the point, this chapter contains such a warning: if we fail to engage in mortifying our sins, we "will die" (Rom. 8:13).

It is for this very reason—to warn of the possibility of apostasy—that John Bunyan inserted at the close of Christian's pilgrimage to the Celestial City the following line: "Then I saw that there was a Way to hell even from the Gates of Heaven, as well as from the City of Destruction."[97]

Can we therefore entertain the assurance of which Paul seems so sure in Romans 8? If *professing* Christians can commit apostasy, must Christians live in uncertainty? The answer lies in the gospel itself and the grace that is at its center.

The gospel in three tenses

We never get past the gospel. What saved us in the past, when we were still in our sins—fallen sons of Adam by nature—was the grace of God in the gospel. Nowhere is that put more succinctly than in Ephesians: "For by grace you have been saved through faith. And this is not your own doing; it is the gift of God, not a result of works, so that no one may boast" (Eph. 2:8–9).

But the New Testament can also speak about our salvation in the present tense—we are "being saved" (1 Cor. 1:18; 2 Cor. 2:15)—as well as in the future tense—we "shall . . . be saved" (Rom. 5:9).

There is only one salvation and one way of salvation. What occurred in our past, works itself out in the present, and comes to consummation in the future is all of a piece. Justification now leads to glorification then (Rom. 8:29–30).

True, some talk unadvisedly about being "saved again," as though salvation could be lost one day and regained the next. In truth, some who speak this way were never saved in the first place. They had made a decision, but it was just that—a human decision and not a sovereign, life-renewing work of the Holy Spirit "from above" (cf. John 3:3, 5). Others who speak this way may have been converted but never acquired the fullness of assurance that should accompany it; when they did, it felt like a new birth all over again.

Empty hands at every stage

Why, then, does the New Testament speak of salvation in three tenses? The answer lies in considering what happens in salvation. Initially, at the point of regeneration, our sins are forgiven—entirely and completely. We have been delivered from sin's penalty. Through faith, we are reckoned to be righteous—as righteous as Christ is. Then, there is sanctification—a process whereby we are being delivered from sin's power. Ultimately, in heaven, we will be delivered from sin's presence. John Stott has argued that when Paul reasoned with Governor Felix about "righteousness and self-control and the coming judgment" (Acts 24:25), he was pointing out the three tenses of salvation.[98]

At every stage—justification, sanctification, glorification— we come with empty hands, seeking mercy from our heavenly Father. Even at the point of our obedience as Christians—we are to "work out [our] salvation with fear and trembling" (Phil. 2:12)—we do so only because God works "in [us], both to will and to work for his good pleasure" (v. 13). And when we enter the Pearly Gates of heaven, wisdom will dictate that we show our empty hands and say with Edward Mote:

> On Christ the solid Rock I stand;
> All other ground is sinking sand.[99]

The moment we drift away from the gospel, we perish. But if we remain on the narrow gospel way, it brings us all the way home.

Postscript

Paul wrote Romans from the house of his friend Gaius[100] during a stay in Corinth. Neither Paul nor the Christians in Rome knew how soon they would need the comfort of Romans 8.

Opinion varies, but many scholars estimate that Romans was written in AD 57–58.[101] Within a decade, many of the Roman Christians to whom the letter was addressed were brutally slaughtered in the Roman amphitheaters. The original readers of Romans faced a terrible dilemma: they could deny Jesus or profess Him knowing that, if they did, they faced certain death. Tacitus' account, written half a century later, and with unmeasured contempt for Nero, is often cited: "Mockery of every sort was added to their deaths. Covered in the skins of beasts, they were torn by dogs and perished, or were nailed to crosses, or doomed to the flames."[102]

Think about it: Paul initially wrote Romans 8 for Christians who had to face the possibility of unspeakably brutal deaths.

Some were crucified in mockery of their faith in Jesus.

Some were mauled to death by wild beasts.

Some were covered in tar and set ablaze.

Paul himself was killed outside the city at *Tre Fontane*.[103] As a Roman citizen, he was spared the horror of crucifixion, being thrown to wild animals, or being burned alive. Most likely, he was beheaded with a sword. "Who shall separate us from the love of Christ? Shall . . . [the] *sword*?" (Rom. 8:35, emphasis added).

No, a sword did not sever Paul from the love of Jesus Christ. Nothing could come between the apostle and the certainty of heaven that awaited him.

The same promise was given to every Roman Christian who died in these appalling circumstances. They knew a love that would not let them go—the love of the Father and of the Son made known by the Holy Spirit, a love that did not spare Jesus.

As a Christian, I am not only "in Christ," but Christ is "in me" (Gal. 2:20). This means, "God's love has been poured into our hearts through the Holy Spirit who has been given to us" (Rom. 5:5). Martyn Lloyd-Jones said, "I am convinced that there is no aspect of Christian truth that has been so sadly neglected in this century."[104]

Oh, the privilege of being a Christian. Can you imagine anything greater than this—that you have been loved from eternity; that "in Christ" you are loved right now?

"O Love that wilt not let me go. . . ."[105]

Endnotes

1   Boice titled a sermon on Romans 8:1–39, an introductory sermon to twenty-seven
     subsequent sermons on Romans 8, "The Greatest Chapter in the Bible." See
     Romans, Vol. 2: The Reign of Grace, Romans 5–8 (Grand Rapids: Baker, 1992), 781.

2   www.fpcjackson.org.

3   J. C. Ryle, *Holiness: Its Nature, Hindrances, Difficulties, and Roots* (Moscow, Ida.:
     Charles Nolan, 2002), 4.

4   From the hymn "And Can It Be That I Should Gain" by Charles Wesley (1738).

5   Jerome, cited in *Nicene and Post-Nicene Fathers, Second Series, Vol. 6: Jerome:
     Letters and Select Works*, eds. Philip Schaff and Henry Wace (Peabody, Mass.: Hen-
     drickson, 2004), 24–25.

6   Nelson Mandela, *Long Walk to Freedom* (London: Abacus, 1994), 673.

7   http://www.cnn.com/2003/SHOWBIZ/10/04/roy.attacked/index.html. Accessed
     Feb. 4, 2010.

8   From the hymn "There is a Green Hill Far Away" by Cecil F. Alexander (1847).

9   *Anselmi Opera Omnia* (Edinburgh: T. Nelson & Sons, 1946–61), I:21.

10   John Calvin, *Institutes of the Christian Religion*, ed. John T. McNeill, trans. Ford
     Lewis Battles, Library of Christian Classics, Vols. 20–21 (Philadelphia: Westminster,
     1960), 3.1.1 (537).

11   Some theologians in the past, by elevating God's will above all other considerations,
     speculated on whether God could simply will the salvation of sinners, *de potentia
     absoluta*. See Carl Trueman, *The Claims of Truth: John Owen's Trinitarian Theology*
     (Exeter: Paternoster, 1998), 149.

12   From the hymn "Rock of Ages" by Augustus Toplady (1776).

13 I understand Romans 7:14–25 in the classical sense of the ongoing struggle of sin in the life of the believer. This also puts a check on the claims of Romans 8. To cite C. E. B. Cranfield, "Thus understood vv. 14–25 bar the way to a complacent, triumphalistic interpretation of Romans 8, into which those who have taken the other view of 7.14ff have often fallen." C. E. B. Cranfield, "Preaching on Romans," in *On Romans and Other New Testament Essays* (Edinburgh: T & T Clark, 1998), 75. See also J. I. Packer, *Keep in Step with the Spirit* (Leicester, England: Inter-Varsity, 1984), 263–70. For an alternative redemptive-historical view, see Dennis E. Johnson, "The Function of Romans 7:13–25 in Paul's Argument for the Law's Impotence and the Spirit's Power, and Its Bearing on the Identity of the Schizophrenic 'I,'" in Lane Tipton and Jeffrey C. Waddington, eds., *Resurrection and Eschatology: Theology in Service of the Church. Essays in Honor of Richard B. Gaffin Jr.* (Phillipsburg, N.J.: P&R, 2008), 3–59.

14 For this view, see Sinclair B. Ferguson, "The Reformed View of Sanctification," in *Christian Spirituality: Five Views of Sanctification* (Downers Grove, Ill.: IVP Academic, 1988), 69.

15 John Owen, *The Works of John Owen*, ed. W. H. Goold (1850–53; repr., London: Banner of Truth, 1965), 275. Hereafter cited as *Works*.

16 John R. W. Stott, *Your Mind Matters* (Downers Grove, Ill.: InterVarsity, 2006), 3ff.

17 Calvin, *Institutes of the Christian Religion*, 1.11.8 (108).

18 Westminster Confession of Faith, 6.4.

19 See Calvin, *Institutes of the Christian Religion*, 2.3.4 (293–94).

20 R. C. Sproul, *Truths We Confess: A Layman's Guide to the Westminster Confession of* Faith (Phillipsburg, N.J.: P&R, 2006), 1:188–89.

21 Sinclair B. Ferguson, *In Christ Alone: Living the Gospel Centered Life* (Orlando, Fla.: Reformation Trust, 2007), 225.

22 Ferguson, *In Christ Alone*, 225.

23 J. I. Packer, *God's Words* (Leicester, England: Inter-Varsity, 1981), 213.

24 Westminster Shorter Catechism, answer to question 38.

25 Not all grammarians agree on the distinction in Greek between the words *heteros* and *allos*, both of which mean "another." I have assumed the view that *heteros* means "another of a *different* kind" and *allos* means "another of the *same* kind." See discussion in D. A. Carson, *The Gospel of John* (Leicester, England: Inter-Varsity; Grand Rapids: Eerdmans, 1991), 266–67, 499–500.

26 James Dobson, in "Family News from Dr. James Dobson," August 1997, cited in a sermon by Geoff Thomas, http://www.alfredplacechurch.org.uk/Sermons /2cor19.htm. Accessed April 30, 2010.

27 Robert Bruce, cited in D. C. MacNicol, *Master Robert Bruce* (Edinburgh: Oliphant Anderson & Ferrier, 1907), 270–71.

28 Owen, *Works*, 6:7. An updated edition of Owen's work on mortification is available; see *Overcoming Sin and Temptation*, eds. Kelly M. Kapic and Justin Taylor (Wheaton, Ill.: Crossway, 2006).

29 J. I. Packer, *A Quest for Godliness: The Puritan Vision of the Christian Life* (Wheaton, Ill.: Crossway, 1994), 194. John "Rabbi" Duncan was professor of Hebrew and Oriental languages at New College in Edinburgh, Scotland, from 1843 to 1870. The discourse by Owen to which he refers is also to be found in *Works*, "On Indwelling Sin in Believers," 6:154–322.

30 Owen, *Works*, 6:24.

31 Owen, *Works*, 6:79.

32 Sinclair B. Ferguson, "The Death of Sin—The Way to Life," in *Inside the Sermon: Thirteen Preachers Discuss Their Methods of Preparing Messages*, ed. Richard Allen Bodey (Grand Rapids: Baker, 1990), 91.

33 Ferguson, *In Christ Alone*, 218. Italics in original.

34 John R. W. Stott, *Message of Galatians* (London: Inter-Varsity; Downers Grove, Ill.: InterVarsity, 1971), 151–52.

35 J. I. Packer, *Knowing God* (Downers Grove, Ill.: InterVarsity, 1973), 202.

36 Calvin, *Institutes of the Christian Religion*, 3.1.3 (540–41).

37 See Douglas J. Moo, *The Epistle to the Romans* (Grand Rapids and Cambridge, England: Eerdmans, 1996), 498.

38 See Galatians 5:25, NIV. See Packer, *Keep in Step with the Spirit*, 11.

39 From the hymn "And Can It Be That I Should Gain" by Charles Wesley (1738).

40 Commentators in the main are not in favor of the view that the phrase "spirit of bondage" refers to the Holy Spirit. See John Murray, *The Epistle to the Romans* (Grand Rapids: Eerdmans, 1968), 1:295–97. For an alternative view, see Charles Hodge, *A Commentary on Romans* (London: Banner of Truth, 1972), 266.

41 Westminster Confession of Faith, 12:1.

42 Sinclair B. Ferguson, *The Holy Spirit* (Downers Grove, Ill.: InterVarsity, 1997), 183.

43 Richard Sibbes, *The Works of Richard Sibbes*, ed. A. B. Grosart (1862–64; repr., Edinburgh: Banner of Truth, 1979–83), 3:456.

44 Owen, *Works*, 4:400.

45 From the song "Man in Black" by Johnny Cash. See also Johnny Cash, *Man in Black: His Own Story in His Own Words* (Grand Rapids: Zondervan, 1975).

46 John Calvin, *Commentaries on the Catholic Epistles*, trans. and ed. John Owen (Grand Rapids: Baker, 1999), 40.

47 See A. A. Hoekema, *The Bible and the Future* (Exeter: Paternoster, 1978), 280.

48 C. S. Lewis, *The Weight of Glory and Other Addresses* (San Francisco: HarperCollins, 2001), 42–44.

49 http://www.ccel.org/bible/phillips/CP06Romans.htm. Accessed March 24, 2010.

50 J. C. Ryle, *Practical Religion* (Cambridge: James Clarke & Co., 1970), 47.

51 Donald Bloesch, *The Struggle of Prayer* (San Francisco: Harper & Row, 1980).

52 http://article.nationalreview.com/267934/god-bless-ted-turner/rod-dreher. Accessed April 30, 2010.

53 Psychoanalytical interpretations of Elijah's mood tend to misread Elijah's prayer. See Dale Ralph Davis, *The Wisdom and the Folly: An Exposition of the Book of First Kings* (Fearn, Ross-shire: Christian Focus, 2002), 257ff.

54 See Moo, *The Epistle to the Romans*, 523n80.

55 See Moo, *The Epistle to the Romans*, 524–25.

56 Ferguson, *The Holy Spirit*, 189.

57 J. I. Packer and Carolyn Nystrom, *Prayer: Finding Our Way Through Duty to Delight* (Downers Grove, Ill.: InterVarsity, 2006), 175.

58 John Calvin, *Commentaries on the Epistle of Paul the Apostle to the Romans*, ed. and trans. John Owen (Grand Rapids: Baker, 2003), 313 (Rom. 8:26).

59 John Piper, *Future Grace* (Leicester, England: Inter-Varsity; Sisters, Ore.: Multnomah Publishers, 1995), 122–23.

60 Westminster Shorter Catechism, answer to Question 11.

61 Herman Ridderbos, *Paul*, trans. John Richard de Witt (Grand Rapids: Eerdmans, 1975), 333.

62 Prosperity gospel writers sometimes suggest that Job was in error when he said these words to his wife, despite the fact that Job 2:10 goes to say, "In all this Job did not sin with his lips."

63 Plato, *Republic*, trans. G. M. A. Grube (Indianapolis: Hackett, 1992), 509b.

64 The sixteenth-century Reformed theologian William Perkins wrote a book based on this passage called *The Golden Chaine*.

65 See Moo, *The Epistle to the Romans*, 532–33.

66 From the hymn "Tis Not That I Did Choose Thee" by Josiah Conder (1836).

67 From the hymn "I Sought the Lord, and Afterward I Knew" (anonymous, 1878).

68 Calvin, *Institutes of the Christian Religion*, 3.21.1 (921).

69 The book was John R. W. Stott's *Basic Christianity*, which recently was published as a fiftieth-anniversary edition (Leicester, England: Inter-Varsity, 2008).

70 John Bunyan, *The Pilgrim's Progress*, ed. W. R. Owen (Oxford: Oxford University Press, 2003), 58.

71 John Owen, *Communion with the Triune God*, eds. Kelly Kapic and Justin Taylor (Wheaton, Ill.: Crossway, 2007), 127–28.

72 See Sinclair B. Ferguson, *A Heart for God* (Edinburgh: Banner of Truth, 1987), 64–65.

73 The hymn "How Great Thou Art" is based on a Swedish poem by Carl Gustav Boberg (1859–1940) and was translated by the British missionary Stuart K. Hine. Hine added the verse referenced here.

74 Octavius Winslow, *No Condemnation in Christ* (Edinburgh: Banner of Truth, 1991), 361.

75 Martin Luther, *Luther's Works* (Weimar edition), xxxvii, 326, cited in C. E. B. Cranfield, *The Gospel of Saint Mark* (Cambridge: Cambridge University Press, 1977), 431.

76 Nicholas Wolterstorff, *Lament for a Son* (Grand Rapids: Eerdmans, 1987), 6. I am indebted to a sermon by Sinclair B. Ferguson on Romans 8:32, delivered at a General Assembly of the Presbyterian Church in America a few years ago, for this illustration.

77 Greg Gilbert, *What Is the Gospel?* (Wheaton, Ill.: Crossway, 2010), 110. Gilbert goes on to point out certain contemporary aberrations that often pass for the gospel, such as "Jesus is Lord," "Creation-Fall-Redemption-Consummation," and "Cultural Transformation." None of these (while true in themselves, though Gilbert has reservations about the idea of cultural transformation as popularly expressed) constitutes "the gospel."

78 Bunyan, *The Pilgrim's Progress*, 58–59.

79 C. H. Spurgeon, *Pictures from Pilgrim's Progress* (Pasadena, Texas: Pilgrim Publications, 1992), 137.

80 Sinclair B. Ferguson, *By Grace Alone* (Orlando, Fla.: Reformation Trust, 2010), 68 and the subsequent discussion on 69–81.

81 Ferguson, *By Grace Alone*, 68.

82 John Howie, *Scots Worthies* (New York: Robert Carter & Brothers, 1853), 425.

83 Calvin, *Institutes of the Christian Religion*, 3.11.1 (726).

84 From the hymn "Approach, My Soul, the Mercy Seat" by John Newton (1779).

85 From the hymn "In Christ Alone" by Stuart Townend and Keith Getty (2001).

86 From the hymn "Faith Reviving" by Augustus Toplady (1772).

87 Elisabeth Elliot, *Shadow of the Almighty: The Life and Testament of Jim Elliot* (San Francisco: Harper, 1989), 108.

88 Packer, *Knowing God*, 250.

89 Cited in E. Michael and Sharon O. Rusten, *The One Year Book of Christian History* (Wheaton, Ill.: Tyndale, 2003), 419.

90 Cf. Moo, *The Epistle to the Romans*, 543n40.

91 The opening lines of the hymn "O Love That Wilt Not Let Me Go" by George Matheson (1882).

92 From the hymn "What Wondrous Love Is This" (anonymous).

93 Cited in Packer, *A Quest for Godliness*, 23.

94 John R. W. Stott writes, "He deliberately uses the perfect tense (*pepeismai*), meaning, 'I have become and I remain convinced,' for the conviction he expresses is rational, settled and unalterable." Stott, *Romans* (Downers Grove, Ill.: InterVarsity, 1994), 258.

95 From the hymn "A Debtor to Mercy Alone" by Augustus Toplady (1740–78).

96 I assume that Paul's words concerning Demas are meant to convey more than just a desertion from the mission in Asia Minor and reflect actual apostasy.

97 Bunyan, *The Pilgrim's Progress*, 154.

98 John R. W. Stott, *The Message of Acts: To the Ends of the Earth* (Leicester, England: Inter-Varsity, 1990), 364.

99 From the hymn "My Hope Is Built on Nothing Less" by Edward Mote (1834).

100 Romans 16:23.

101 See Donald Guthrie, *New Testament Introduction*, Revised Edition (Leicester, England: Apollos; Downers Grove, Ill.: InterVarsity, 1990), 406–8. For an earlier date (AD 55), see, for example, Leon Morris' discussion, *The Epistle to the Romans* (Leicester, England: Inter-Varsity; Grand Rapids: Eerdmans, 1988), 5–7.

102 Tacitus, *Annals*, 15:44, cited in Ivor J. Davidson, *The Birth of the Church*, Vol. 1 of *The Baker History of the Church*, ed. Tim Dowley (Grand Rapids: Baker, 2004), 192.

103 Assuming the unreliability of Eusebius' historiography, the best date for Paul's martyrdom is AD 64, barely six years later. See discussion in Guthrie, *New Testament Introduction*, 1001–10.

104 Cited in Iain Murray, *Lloyd-Jones: Messenger of Grace* (Edinburgh: Banner of Truth, 2008), 210.

105 The opening of the hymn "O Love That Wilt Not Let Me Go" by George Matheson (1882).

Scripture Index

Genesis
3:1 — 120
3:3 — 120
3:17–19 — 70
22:12 — 110
50:20 — 96

Exodus
3:14 — 63
3:15 — 63
18:22 — 85
34:7 — 10

Numbers
6:24–26 — 21
11:17 — 85

1 Kings
19:4 — 84

Job
1:21 — 97
2:10 — 97, 146
35:12 — 64

Psalms
3:5 — 64
14:1–3 — 24
14:3 — 24
44:22 — 135
56:2–3 — 107
56:9 — 107

Proverbs
14:12 — 21

Ecclesiastes
1:2–3 — 69

Isaiah
64:4 — 75
65:17 — 68, 74
66:22 — 68, 74

Amos
1:3 — 122
1:6 — 122
1:9 — 122
1:11 — 122

About the Author

Dr. Derek W. H. Thomas is the associate minister at First Presbyterian Church in Columbia, South Carolina, and an adjunct professor of systematic theology at Reformed Theological Seminary. He is a council member of the Alliance of Confessing Evangelicals, which he also serves as editorial director and as editor of *Reformation21*, the Alliance's online magazine.

A native of Wales, Dr. Thomas graduated from RTS in 1978, then pastored for seventeen years in Belfast, Northern Ireland. He earned his PhD from the University of Wales, Lampeter. He served as the minister of teaching at First Presbyterian Church in Jackson, Mississippi, before his call to Columbia.

He has written numerous books, including *The Storm Breaks: Job Simply Explained*; *Wisdom: The Key to Living God's Way*; and *Praying the Savior's Way*, based on the Lord's Prayer. He also co-edited *Give Praise to God: A Vision for Reforming Worship*. His interests include the music of Anton Bruckner, Richard Wagner, and Gustav Mahler, and he has a passion for good coffee.

Dr. Thomas and his wife, Rosemary, have been married for almost thirty-five years. They have two adult children and two grandchildren, Hannah and Daniel.